The Commonsense of Wine

André L. Simon, C.B.E.

From a portrait by the late James Gunn
presented to The Wine and Food Society by
the members on M. Simon's 83rd birthday in 1960.

André L. Simon

THE COMMONSENSE OF WINE

Foreword by André Maurois

The Wine and Food Society

MICHAEL JOSEPH

A Publication of
The Wine and Food Society Limited
2 Hyde Park Place, London, W. 2.

President: André L. Simon

Consultant Editor: André L. Simon

M. 31-8-66

The book was designed and produced by
George Rainbird Limited,
2 Hyde Park Place, London, W. 2.

The type was composed by Graphic Film Limited, Dublin,
Republic of Ireland; the paper was supplied by Matthäus
Salzers Söhne, Vienna 9, Austria; the binding material was
supplied by Balamundi Nederland N.V., Huizen, Holland;
the book was printed and bound in Hungary by Athenaeum
Printing Works, Budapest.

CONTENTS

FOREWORD

Great wines are treated with respect in France. A certain ceremony applies where tasting is concerned and in the cellars of any well-known vintner, the moment of judgment passes in silence. Afterwards the guests describe their impressions gravely and in colourful phraseology. "Il a du panorama" says one. "Il a le chapeau sur l'oreille" suggests another. I remember having been innocent enough to ask a Bordelais who was served a formidable Premier Crû from a magnum, "Is the wine better served in this way?" He replied indulgently, "If there were two different bottles, all conversation would become impossible".

He was right. The real connoisseurs take as much pleasure in talking about wine in nicely shaded conversations as they do in drinking it. In wine they describe and savour a work of art, and in this way French wines have exercised and continue to exercise a benevolent influence on the culture of those who love them. Wine has inspired poets, helped diplomats and civilised everyday life. Everything, however, that is perfect in itself calls for other forms of perfection, great wines demand great cooking and the excellence of the dining table demands fine wines. The closer the great vineyards, the higher the civilisation.

The vineyards of France are to our eyes a national heritage like our châteaux and our gardens, like French fashion and French painting. Only a long tradition and the devoted love of patient growers has brought their product to this pitch of excellence. Our friends abroad know this and some of them are as dedicated and as wise in wine as the best *Maîtres de chai*. No ambassador, for instance, who is made a Chevalier du Tastevin or a Jurat de St. Emilion will have earned it because of his position but because of his competence.

To André Simon, above all, we are grateful for having been for so many years the ambassador of the wines of France.

ANDRÉ MAUROIS

PREFACE

There is nowadays a great deal more to know, to do, and to see than ever before, but not a day, an hour, or a minute more, which is why there are people who will cheat hunger with a biscuit, a sandwich or a few drinks to 'save time'. What folly!

Whatever your ambition, profession or avocation may be, what matters most is to be fit and to keep fit; it cannot be done by drugs or diet: we must enjoy our meals daily and sound sleep nightly.

Meals are an inescapable necessity, but they must never be allowed to become dull, monotonous, a chore instead of the tonic and the joy that they should be and can so easily be. Pleasant company at mealtime makes all the difference, and there is pleasant company to be had for the asking – and a few coins – in a bottle of good wine on the table.

Food that is partnered with the right wine tastes better, we enjoy it more, it is digested better and it does us more good. No meal is ever dull when there is wine to drink and talk about.

There may be either less or more alcohol in beer or spirits than there is in wine, but what is of so much greater importance than alcohol is the fact that there are varieties of wines beyond count, so that it is always possible to find the wine that will best suit us and the fare, the company, the occasion and the mood of the day.

We all have different finger-prints so that we expect to have also different taste buds. Nobody has the monopoly of good taste and there are so many different wines, of all shades of red and gold, of all ages, of all countries, that it is great fun to hunt for and find those wines which happen to appeal to one's own taste more than any of the others at different times.

It is quite obvious that most people have not got the time to learn all that there is to know about vineyards, wines and vintages or about the care and service of wine. They need not know much or indeed anything about wine to enjoy it, but there are nevertheless many who would like to know where the wine in their glasses came from, what sort of people made it, when, and how it was made and bottled.

Wine is a work of art with many facets: it is well worth talking about

11

for people with inquisitive and cultured minds, and they will surely value a friend, not at the other end of the telephone, but on their own bookshelf, with the right answer to any of their questions.

This is exactly what this book, I hope, will be and do. All that I have learnt in the course of the four score years during which I have loved wine, has been the making of this book. I have done my best to answer all the questions which I have ever asked myself, and the questions which a great many people have asked me about wine during my long and well-wined life.

ANDRÉ L. SIMON

THE WINE CONNOISSEUR

Q. **What is a connoisseur?**

A. A connoisseur is a person of taste who is blessed with a critical sense of appreciation: one who looks for and enjoys all that is beautiful, interesting and genuine.

Q. **What is a connoisseur of wine?**

A. A wine connoisseur is a connoisseur who takes an intelligent interest in wine, who does not grudge the money that it costs to buy, and who enjoys drinking it and talking about it with friends.

Q. **How does one become a connoisseur of wine?**

A. To become a wine connoisseur one must possess normal, sound senses of sight, smell and taste and use them all sensibly – that is, taking a good look at the wine in the glass before drinking it, making sure that it *looks* right – clear and true of colour, whether it be golden, ruby or tawny; then taking a good smell of the wine in the glass, making sure that it *smells* right – that is pleasant, flowery and, above all, free from any trace of mustiness or any other objectionable smell; and lastly, taking a good sip of the wine, making sure that it *tastes* right – *clean,* whether dry or sweet, that is to say free from any odd taste or flavour. The wine connoisseur who drinks with care and appreciation not much wine but many different wines will soon be able to tell which are fair, fine, or great, *ordinaires* or *très ordinaires*. What is more difficult, as well as very important, is to drink different wines with a sufficient measure of concentration to develop a wine memory – that is, the faculty of recognising the name and vintage of a wine which one has had before.

Q. **Does this cost a great deal?**

A. Certainly not. There is no obligation for a wine connoisseur to have a long purse any more than a red nose. It is variety and not quantity which is necessary for the education of taste buds, and there are any number of different wines available at quite reasonable prices from nearby France or far away Australia; from Italy, Spain, Portugal and Germany; Hungary, Austria, Switzerland and Yugoslavia; Cyprus, Turkey and South Africa; even from California and Chile, and from China and Japan.

Q. **Are books on wine of real help?**

A. Yes, they are. They tell the wine connoisseur what to look for in a wine and they help him to choose the right wine, just as the signpost helps the traveller to choose the right road. Obviously, the wine in the glass matters much more than the wine in the book, just as the petrol in the car's tank matters more than the signpost, but both the book and the signpost can save a great deal of time and trouble.

Q. **Does the connoisseur of wine take much interest in food as well as wine?**

A. Indeed, he does. The connoisseur of wine prefers it to hard liquor and soft drinks. Wine is never better than with food, nor does food ever taste better than with wine, the right wine.

Q. **Which is the right wine with the right food?**

A. It is a matter of personal taste and nobody has the monopoly of good taste. There is, however, such a thing as bad taste in wine and food as in dress and speech and all else, and there are wines which are generally considered as 'right' with certain foods.

Q. **Which are the best wines to serve with Hors d'Oeuvre?**

A. Most Hors d'Oeuvre being spicy, oily and/or vinegary, the younger and cheaper wines are more suitable than any great vintage wine, which may be served later with the main course. The wine connoisseur would choose the kind of wine likely to 'lead up' to the better wine to come, maybe a youthful Beaujolais if a fine Burgundy is to follow; an even younger Moselle if one of the great Hocks is to be next; a Bordeaux *Bourgeois* if one of the Médoc *Grands Crus* is to come later.

Q. **Which is the right wine to serve with soup?**

A. Soup should be served piping hot if it is to call forth the stomach's gastric juices ready to cope with the solid food to follow. Hence iced Champagne or any iced wine must never be drunk immediately after hot soup. A fairly dry Sherry or Madeira, not chilled, is best.

Q. **Is it right to serve Hors d'Oeuvre and soup at the same meal?**

A. It is like publishing a book with an Introduction and a Preface! The *Cuisine Classique* favours Hors d'Oeuvre for the *Déjeuner*, and no soup; soup for the *Dìner*, and no Hors d'Oeuvre.

Q. **Which is the right wine to serve with fish?**

A. All white wines are more suitable than red, but it is only common sense to partner fish and wine of similar quality; a Muscadet or Sylvaner d'Alsace, for instance, with boiled cod or fried plaice; Chablis *Grand Cru* or a fine Mittel Mosel with a sole or trout; Champagne or Bâtard-Montrachet with lobster or salmon.

Q. **Which wines are best with butcher's meat?**

A. Red wines are best with butcher's meat but it is a rule with many exceptions. Whereas no red wine tastes well with fish, many white wines will taste very well with meat.

Q. **Which wines are best with poultry?**

A. The choice of wine to serve with poultry does not depend so much on the bird as on its garnishings or method of cooking. White wine, for instance, will be best with a *Poulet à l'ancienne*, a poached chicken served with cream, but a red wine will be best with a *Coq au vin*, which is cooked in red wine and *flambé* with brandy, or with a *Poulet chasseur*, whilst a *vin rosé* could be served with a *Poulet Maryland* or a *Poulet à l'Indienne*, the first having bananas in its garniture and the other some curry powder in its sauce.

Q. **Which wines are best with game?**

A. Red wines certainly partner game better than white wines, and the wine connoisseur usually chooses a fine Claret to serve with grouse or partridge, a fine red Burgundy with pheasant or hare, and an Hermitage or Châteauneuf-du-Pape with snipe or woodcock.

Q. **Which wines are best with cheese?**

A. Cheese, wrote Grimod de la Reynière, is the *Biscuit des Ivrognes*, meaning that one will enjoy wine more and will drink more wine with cheese than with any other kind of food. The choice of wine with cheese is chiefly a matter of taste, supplies and tradition. In Switzerland, for instance, a cheese country *par excellence*, they drink mostly white wines with cheese because they make so many more and so much better white wines than red. The same applies to Germany, whilst in France most people prefer red wine with cheese, and in England Port is more popular than any other wine with cheese.

Q. **Which wines are best with the dessert or last course?**

A. It all depends on what the last course happens to be but, as a rule, it includes some confectionery or sweet pudding or ice-cream, and the best wines to serve are the rich Sauternes, *Spätlese* Hocks, Coteaux du Layon and such sweet white wines. Champagne Demi-Sec is sweeter and better than the Champagne Extra Sec with sweets but it is practically impossible to get it in England. With fresh fruit, almost any fruit with the exception of pineapple – good as it is to eat, it is sure to ruin any wine – Port, Sherry and Madeira are best.

Q. **What about savouries?**

A. A savoury is to a meal what a postscript is to a letter: a parting, last thought. Savouries are small, mostly highly seasoned, and always tasty morsels which come when the appetite is gone but when there is still a glass of wine to drink and a story to tell. With savouries of the chicken liver, bacon, mushroom and cheese types any good red wine will be most acceptable, but, naturally, a chilled white wine will partner more happily all fishy savouries from the humble sardine on toast to the sporty Angel on Horseback.

Q. **What is wine?**

A. Wine is the suitably fermented juice of ripe fresh grapes.

Q. **What is fermentation?**

A. Fermentation is a natural, not to say inevitable phenomenon responsible for grape-juice or *must* becoming wine. Fermentation was a mystery and a puzzle all through the centuries until Pasteur, only a little more than a century ago, proved that it was due to the presence and nature of living yeasts which could be encouraged or checked, or destroyed at will according to the wine the wine-maker wished to make.

Q. **What is the meaning of pasteurisation?**

A. Pasteurisation is the raising of the temperature of a newly made wine to a degree sufficient to kill and render inactive any remaining yeasts which might be a menace.

Q. **Are wines better when they have been pasteurised?**

A. They are not better, they are safer; they will not turn to vinegar nor go 'out of condition', but they will never be truly great.

Q. **Is chaptalisation the same as pasteurisation?**

A. Not in the least. Chaptal was another Frenchman, Napoleon's Minister of Agriculture, who was anxious to encourage the culture of the sugar-beet and the making of beet-sugar, in France, at a time, during the Napoleonic Wars, when cane sugar could no longer reach France from her West Indies Islands. Chaptal recommended the use of beet-sugar added to grape-juice, at the time of the vintage, to raise the alcoholic degree of wines and increase their keeping quality.

Q. **Are the wines which are chaptalised any better?**

A. They are not; they are not so good, but they are stronger.

Q. **Is wine any better than other beverages?**

A. Yes, it certainly is the best of all beverages.

Q. **Why?**

A. Because it is purer than water, safer than milk, plainer than soft drinks, gentler than spirits, nimbler than beer, and ever so much more pleasant to the educated senses of sight, smell and taste than any of the other drinkable liquids known to us.

Q. **Which are the chief varieties of wine?**

A. The varieties of wine are beyond count, not only because there is every year a new tide of all kinds of wines flowing in from all the vineyards of the world, but also because the wines made from the grapes of those same vineyards in previous years change for better or worse with age. There are, however, three main great classes or divisions of wine called *Table Wines*, *Sparkling Wines* and *Fortified Wines*. The table wines are the beverage wines, with as little as 8° of alcohol or as much as 13°: they are mostly inexpensive wines, thirst-quenching and health-giving, with no claim to any particularly attractive *bouquet* or *finesse*. There is, however, a fair quantity of table wine which is distinctly better than the rest. These wines possess a taste and vinous appeal of their own; they are made with greater care and they cost appreciably more. Lastly, there is a very small percentage of table wines made now and again, in particularly favourable years and nowhere else but in France and Germany, which are not merely good or very good wines, but great wines. They are the aristocrats among the wines of Bordeaux, Burgundy and the Rhineland vineyards, and there is never enough of them, although their cost is often called prohibitive.

Q. **What about sparkling wines?**
A. There are quite a number of different sparkling wines made in most, if not actually all, the vinelands of the world. In all sparkling wine the carbonic acid gas to which they owe their effervescence is the same, but the quality of the wine itself varies greatly from the sweetest and cheapest to the driest and most expensive of the best vintage Champagne.

Q. **What about the fortified wines?**
A. They also differ greatly in quality and cost. All of them are wines of appreciably higher alcoholic strength than table wines or sparkling wines. They are wines to which some brandy has been added during or after fermentation. Some are served before meals to provoke the flow of gastric juices and stimulate appetite: Sherry is the prototype of those preprandial wines. Others are dessert wines, served at the end or after a meal; they are valued for their comforting warmth and they help digestion as well as conversation. Port is the prototype of after-dinner wines.

Q. **Which are the chief reasons responsible for the differences in the style and quality of all kinds of wine?**
A. Differences in the style and quality, hence also the cost, of all wines are due to a number of causes, of which the four most important are:
(1) The vines, of which there are many varieties.
(2) The nature of the soil and sub-soil of the vineyards: also their aspect and elevation.

(3) Climatic conditions – that is, the hours of sunshine and inches of rain, and their incidence, from year to year.

(4) The degree of professional skill, honesty, means, pride and ambition of the men who grow the grapes and make the wine.

Q. **Which are the countries where wines are made?**

A. All the civilised countries of the world where the climatic conditions – that is, sunshine and rain at the right times – make it possible to grow wine-making grapes in the open with a fair chance that their grapes will ripen most years, if not every year.

Q. **Which are the more important wine-producing countries of the world?**

A. In Europe they are France, Italy, Spain, Portugal, U.S.S.R., Rumania, Yugoslavia, Germany, Hungary, Austria, Greece and the Greek Islands, Czechoslovakia, Switzerland, Bulgaria and Turkey. In North America, the United States, Mexico and Canada. In South America, Argentina, Brazil, Chile and Uruguay. In North Africa, Algeria, Morocco, Tunisia and Egypt. In South Africa, the Cape Province. In Australia, Victoria, New South Wales and South Australia.

Q. **Are there any vineyards in England?**

A. Yes, a few in Hampshire, Surrey, Sussex and maybe elsewhere, where a little wine is made experimentally or as a hobby, but not as a commercial proposition.

Q. **Why?**

A. Because the English climate is so uncertain that grapes grown in the open are not likely to ripen fully more than one year in five.

Q. **Are there any wine connoisseurs in England?**

A. Certainly, and maybe more than anywhere else.

Q. **How can this be?**

A. Because in wine-producing countries the people drink their local wines as a matter of course, rarely if ever being given the opportunity, or having even the wish, to compare them with other wines, the wines of other lands such as are commonly available in England.

Q. **Which are the wines mostly in demand in England?**

A. They are the table wines and sparkling wines of France – the wines of Bordeaux, Burgundy and Champagne, also the wines of the Loire and the Rhône, of Alsace and Provence; the still and sparkling Hocks and Moselles of Germany; table wines from Italy, Spain, Portugal, Switzerland, Yugoslavia, Greece, Austria and Luxembourg. Also the table wines and fortified wines of Australia and South Africa. But the greatest demand for any one wine is for Sherry, the most popular of the fortified wines from Spain. Next come Port and Madeira, wines which no longer enjoy the same measure of popular favour which was their privilege for many years; they are again, however, in great and growing demand. It is also possible to buy, occasionally, many other wines which are not commonly available from the majority of wine merchants, such as Turkish, Russian, Californian, Chilean, New Zealand, Chinese and Japanese wines.

WINE BOTTLES, DECANTERS AND GLASSES

Q. **Are all wine bottles made of glass?**

A. The wine bottles of today are all glass bottles of different size, shape, and colour, but all through the Middle Ages, in England, the standard wine bottle was made of leather: it was filled from the cask, at the tavern, for use in the home or on the road, hooked on a rider's saddle or the cart driver's seat. The leather bottle was unbreakable.

Q. **When were glass bottles first made in England?**

A. Glass bottles were first made in England, chiefly in the Weald and East Sussex, in Tudor times, but they did not come into fairly general use until Stuart times. They were made of blackish-green glass, with a bulbous body, a long neck, at first, and soon after with more spheric body and a very short neck. They stood up on table or shelf but they could not lie on their side.

Q. **When were wine bottles made as we know them today?**

A. The cylindrical wine bottles of today were first made during the second half of the eighteenth century, when corkscrews first came into general use and cork stoppers were first used as we still use them now. The cylindrical shape of the wine bottle was then evolved to make it possible to bin away bottled wine and leave it alone and in peace to mature slowly in a deep, dark, damp, cold cellar.

Q. **Must a wine cellar be deep?**

A. A deep cellar is better for wine because it is less likely to be susceptible to changes of temperature: it is not good for wine to be hot in summer and cold in winter.

Q. **What difference does it make to the wine?**

A. Heat expands and cold contracts, which interferes with the smooth ripening or maturing of the bottled wine.

Q. **Why should a cellar be dark and damp?**

A. Darkness is desirable because light does affect the colour of the wine, more particularly the colour of red wines. A damp cellar is no better than a dry one for the wine, but it is better for the corks: their worst enemy, the weevil, a horrid little boring grub, hates damp.

Q. **What is the legal wine measure for wine in the U.K. and the U.S.A?**

A. The standard wine measure in both countries is the Gallon which holds four quarts, but, in the U.K., the gallon holds 160 fluid ounces (277·42 cubic inches) and the legal or 'Imperial' quart holds 40 fluid ounces, whereas in the U.S.A. the gallon holds 128 fluid ounces and the quart 32. Wines, however, which wine-merchants sell in both countries are bottled in smaller bottles than the standard quarts: they are known as 'reputed quarts'.

Q. **Why is there a difference between the capacity of the U.K. quart and that of the U.S.A?**

A. For no better reason, apparently, than that in England, somebody, in 1824, considered that it was time for a change, and the Americans did not see why they should do the same: so their gallon and quart are still the same as in England during Queen Anne's reign.

Q. **Which is the wine bottle mostly in use in the U.K. and the U.S.A?**

A. It is the reputed quart bottle which holds 26·66 fluid ounces in the U.K., and 25·60 in the U.S.A. or 6 to the gallon instead of 4.

Q. **Which are the wine bottles smaller than the quart?**

A. The pint, or half quart, is the more commonly used for bottled wines: there are some imperial pints made (8 to the gallon) for Champagne, but most pints are half the reputed quart or 12 to the gallon. There are also quarter bottles made (24 to the gallon).

Q. **Which are the wine bottles larger than the quart?**

A. The only bottle that is made to a large extent is the Magnum: it holds 2 reputed quarts or 3 to the gallon. Magnums are made in small quantities for all still wines and in much larger quantities for Champagne. They also make, almost exclusively for Champagne, a number of larger bottles such as the Jeroboam (2 Magnums), Rehoboam (3 Magnums), Methuselah (4 Magnums), Salmanazar (6 Magnums), Balthazar (8 Magnums), and Nebuchadnezzar (10 Magnums). In Bordeaux, fine Claret is sometimes bottled in a large bottle known as *Impériale* which holds about $8\frac{1}{2}$ reputed quarts. In Scotland, Port was sometimes bottled in a large bottle called a Tregnum holding 3 reputed quarts; also in a larger bottle called a Tappit-Hen, holding about 3 imperial quarts.

Q. **Are the larger bottles better for the wine lodged in them?**

A. It depends upon the type of wine and the length of time spent in the cellar. Champagne, for instance, is no better in an outsize bottle because the wine has to be decanted to fill the big bottle and the sooner a decanted wine is drunk, after decanting, the better. On the other hand, Claret, Burgundy or Port will age more slowly and more graciously if left for a long while in the peace of the cellar lodged in a Magnum or an outsize bottle.

Q. **Which is the standard wine bottle in France?**

A. In France the standard wine measure is the litre of 35·19 fluid ounces (U.K.) and 33·78 fluid ounces (U.S.A). In France, the litre is also the bottle most used for bottling and marketing *ordinaires* wines, the red and the white plain table wines, about 90% of the total home consumption. Litre bottles are nearly always made of white glass. The quality table wines are always bottled in smaller bottles of different shapes but usually of 0·75 litre which is practically the same as the reputed quart of the U.K. and the U.S.A. The Bordeaux bottle is used for a great many other quality wines besides those of Bordeaux; the body is cylindrical, it has shoulders, a short neck, and a punt: white wines are bottled in white glass bottles, and red wines in dark green glass bottles. The Burgundy bottle is made of dark green glass for both the red and the white wines: the body is cylindrical but rather 'fatter' than that of the Bordeaux bottle, it has no shoulders, the neck gradually slopes expandingly to become the body. The Champagne bottle is also usually made of dark green glass and in the same shape as the Burgundy bottle but it is made of thicker glass and is a good deal heavier. There are now Champagne bottles made by some Champagne shippers for the marketing of their best Cuvées with longer necks and fancy shaped bodies, but their wine content is the same. In Alsace, the wines are bottled in blue-green, thin and long cylindrical bottles similar to those used for bottling the wines of the Moselle, Saar and Ruwer. In Provence, they bottle and market their wines in a bottle of peculiar shape and made of white glass. There is nothing to stop anybody designing different wine bottles, but it is desirable that quarts should hold the usual 26·66 fluid ounces, and the pints 13·33 fluid ounces; also that their shape allows the bottles to be binned horizontally.

Q. **What is the standard wine measure in Germany?**
A. The litre is the standard wine measure, in Germany, but all quality wines are bottled and marketed in smaller bottles of different shapes and colours which hold practically the same as the reputed quart and reputed pint in the U.K. and the U.S.A. The most typically German wine bottle is the *Bocksbeutel*, a flat-sided flask or flagon, now made of green glass, but originally made of brick-red glass. It is probably derived from the ancient *costre,* or pilgrim's flask which had one or two small rings or lugs for rope or leatherbrace. These bottles are used solely for the wines of Franconia, and also in a small district of Baden for the *Mauer Weine.* The wines of the Rhineland and Moselle are bottled and marketed in long, thin bottles which are made of brick-red glass for all Hocks, and of blue-green glass for the wines of the Moselle, Saar and Ruwer.

Q. **Which is the standard wine measure in Italy?**
A. It is the litre, which is rarely used, however, for bottling wine. Most quality red wines are bottled in bottles similar to the Bordeaux bottle, except in Tuscany where the *Fiasco* is used instead of the

Bottiglia. The Tuscan *Fiasco* is really a Magnum: it holds 2 reputed quarts (53·32 ounces): it is made of white, thin glass, protected by artistically matted straw. The *Mezzo Fiasco* or half *Fiasco* is in much greater use than the *Fiasco*. The wine of Montepulciano is usually bottled in *Fiaschi* smaller than those of Tuscany: they are known as *Pulcianelli*.

Q. **Are all wine bottles labelled?**
A. Today all quality wines are labelled.

Q. **Has it not always been so?**
A. Certainly not. Labels were used for the first time in the eighteenth century for Champagne, and some time after for the Hocks and Moselles, but for no other wines. From then on, however, the custom of labelling spread and is now universal.

Q. **Was there any reason for this?**
A. The reason was that Champagne and German wines were served from their own bottles, but the bottles of other wines were not seen on the table: their wines were always decanted.

Q. **Is decanting good or bad for the wine?**
A. Decanting is good for all wines except sparkling wines. Old wines with a sediment are in much better condition if carefully decanted than if served from a 'cradle'; the air also gives their bouquet a better chance to come out. And all wines, old or young, look so much better in a plain or cut-glass decanter than in a wine bottle however plastered with labels it may be.

Q. **Is there a reason why wines are no longer decanted as much as they were formerly?**
A. There are two main reasons. The first is that there are very few people left nowadays who have the time and the inclination to sit at table after dinner for hours, talking and arguing and drinking Port, Madeira or Brown Sherry, wines which had to be in decanters to be handed round the table time after time. The second is that in our modern age of intense publicity, bottles are being used, as they never were before, to advertise the name of the wine, its shippers, its vintage, how sweet or dry it is meant to be, the awards it has won

24

in competitions, the royal or distinguished people who bought some of it, and so on.

Q. **How were wines identified before labels were used?**

A. By coloured wax. Every cellarman had a brass pot, like a glue pot, in which he melted wax, black, red, dark or light blue, yellow, green, etc., in which he just dipped the top of each newly filled bottle so as to cover and protect its cork. He could, and often did, stamp on to the wax the date of the vintage or the initials of the firm. When the wine was sold, it was invoiced with the colour of the wax duly recorded as well as the description of the wine, and the customer or his butler recorded in the home Cellar Book all such details: identification was thus perfectly easy.

Q. **How were wines identified when in decanters?**

A. They were identified by little silver, enamel, ivory, mother-of-pearl and other 'labels' or tickets which were suspended by a silver chain from the neck of the decanter: each one of those little labels or tickets bore the name of a wine, or its initial like a capital P for Port, S for Sherry, and so on; there were a number of such chained labels or tickets to choose from according to the wine in the decanter.

Glasses

Q. **Which are the best wine glasses?**

A. The best wine glasses are those with a bowl of the finest and purest white glass: they give every wine the best chance to show off its beautiful colour.

Q. **Are there not some beautiful coloured glasses?**

A. There are some very beautiful Salviati Venetian glasses and Slovak cut-glass coloured glasses: they also made in England in early Victorian times wine glasses with all the colours of the rainbow, all of them, however, unfair to wine, hence unsuitable as wine glasses.

Q. **Should wine glasses be large or small?**

A. Neither too large nor too small: the 4-ounce glass is best when there is only one glass used. On festive occasions, when a sequence of wines is to be served, three glasses of different height and size are best, a 3-ounce glass for Sherry, Port and Madeira, a 4-ounce glass for any of the red and white table wines, and a 5-ounce glass for Champagne.

Q. **How big are the 3-, 4-, and 5-ounce glasses?**

A. The ordinary or reputed quart wine bottle holds 26 liquid ounces so that a bottle will fill eight 3-ounce glasses, six 4-ounce glasses, and about five 5-ounce glasses, that is if filled as wine glasses ought to be filled, 1 inch from the brim for the smaller glasses, and 1½ inches from the brim for the larger ones, thus giving one's nose a chance to enjoy the wine's *bouquet* before it reaches the taste buds.

Q. **Does the shape of the glass also matter?**

A. It does, but ancient tradition and changing fashions are mostly responsible for the shape of glasses used for different wines, more particularly Champagne and Hock.

Q. **Which is the best Champagne glass?**

A. The best Champagne glass is, like the best Champagne, the one that you happen· to like best. But from Queen Anne to Queen Victoria, that is during the whole of the eighteenth century and the first half of the nineteenth, the universally accepted Champagne glass, in England as well as in France, was the *Flûte*, a tall and narrow stemless glass, with a flat foot, holding a minimum of wine and a maximum of bubbles. It was superseded a hundred years ago by the *Coupe*, a deep saucer stuck on a cut-glass or plain stem which held a maximum of wine and a minimum of bubbles.

Q. **Which is the right Champagne glass, Flûte or Coupe?**

A. Both are equally unsuitable for Champagne. The glasses which hold a more sensible quantity of wine than the *Flûte*, and keep the bubbles in the wine longer, are the *Tulipe* and the *Ballon*; the first is somewhat like a half-opened tulip on a tall plain, or cut-glass, stem; the other is somewhat like the lower half of a little balloon cut in two; the brims of both these glasses are slightly incurved.

Q. **Which is the best Hock glass?**

A. Hock and all German wines will taste just as good in any fine glass with a bowl of fair size and pure whiteness, but they will look better when served in typically German glasses.

Q. **Which is the most typically German glass?**
A. The most typically German glass is known as the *Römer,* a name which, some people suggest, indicates that it was introduced by the Romans nearly two thousand years ago. It certainly was in use in Germany during the past three hundred years: the bowl, cup-like with an incurved brim, used to be coloured, mostly in different shades of green, and it stood on a short stumpy pillar-like stem which was often decorated with applied glass bosses, very small and of no special design or significance. Today's *Römer* has a white bowl, a taller and more elegant pillar-like stem with more artistic small decorations, technically known as 'prunts', *Nuppen* in German.

Q. **Is the Römer the only typically German wine glass?**
A. It is not: there are different Rhine and Moselle wine glasses which are the tallest of all glasses on a dining room table: their bowl may be tulip or cup in shape, just a little incurved at the brim, of clear plain or white cut-glass, and with a very tall stem, plain or cut, white or coloured. In the days of Queen Victoria, Hock glasses were always coloured glasses, pretty enough to look at but making it impossible to look at the wine.

Q. **Are there any special glasses made for different wines other than Champagne and German wines?**
A. In the Val de Loire, they drink their white wines from a tall glass, as tall as a Hock glass, but with a straight-sided square cup instead of a curved and rounded one; and in Spain, they drink Sherry from a *Copita,* a white 'funnel' glass, an ideal tasting glass, the facsimile, in size and shape, of the terracotta Roman glasses of two thousand years ago. Modern glass manufacturers make many different sets of wine glasses of various designs and sizes, the smallest of the sets being invariably the glass which they call the 'Port' glass, a 2-ounce glass or even smaller, which is so unfair to both the Port and the drinker thereof. Claret and Burgundy, as well as white wines other than Hock, should have a 4-ounce glass or larger, which, when three parts filled and no more, gives one a chance to test, taste and enjoy a fine wine.

27

Q. **Is the choice of the glass really important?**

A. Indeed, it is very important. A fine glass helps us to appreciate and enjoy the colour, the bouquet and the 'feel' of a wine at the lips. Which is why it is also very important to use a clean cloth, never used for anything else, after glasses have been washed, to dry them and polish them. Brand new glasses, straight from the makers, may be as clean as a new pin, but they *must* be washed; otherwise, the first wine in them will smell of packing paper.

The Fluid Ounce Content of Various Wine Bottles in the U.K. and U.S.A.

	U.K.	U.S.A.
U.K. Gallon	160·00	153·60
American Gallon	133·33	128·00
Imperial Quart	40·00	38·40
American Quart	33·33	32·00
U.K. Reputed Quart (0·75 litre)	26·66	25·60
U.S.A. Reputed Quart (4/5)	26·66	25·60
Imperial Pint	20·00	19·20
American Pint	16·665	16·00
U.K. Reputed Pint	13·33	12·80
U.S.A. Reputed Pint	13·33	12·80
U.K. Magnum	53·33	51·20
U.S.A. Magnum	53·33	51·20

British and French Wine Measures

Gallons	Litres	Litres	Gallons
1	4·54	1	0·22
2	9·09	2	0·44
3	13·63	3	0·66
4	18·17	4	0·88
5	22·72	5	1·10
6	27·26	6	1·32
7	31·80	7	1·54
8	36·36	8	1·76
9	40·89	9	1·98
10	45·43	10	2·20

FRANCE

Q. **Is France the greatest of the world's vinelands?**

A. There are more acres in Italy than in France where grapes grow, and there is more wine made in Italy than in France in some years, but France may rightly claim to be the greatest of the world's vinelands. Her vineyards have produced for centuries, as they do now, a greater quantity as well as a greater variety of fine wines than the vineyards of all other wine-producing countries.

Q. **How much wine can the vineyards of France produce in a year?**

A. When they escape spring frosts and when the sun smiles upon them they can produce up to 1,600,000,000 gallons[1] of wine which is divided, accordingly to French official statistics, into three classes known, in France, and in the wine trade, by the initials A.C., V.D.Q.S. and V.C.C.

A.C. stands for *Appellations contrôlées*, roughly 135 million gallons of the best wines; V.D.Q.S. stands for *Vins délimités de qualité supér ieure*, roughly 130 million of the next best wines; V.C.C. stands for *Vins de consommation courante*, roughly, 1,235 million gallons or 82% of the total; they are the more homely of *ordinaires* wines.

Q. **Are all A.C. wines fine quality wines?**

A. They are all genuine wines, entitled to the regional name which they bear and made according to rules laid down to ensure their right alcoholic strength, but the proportion of really fine, let alone great, wines among the A.C. wines is very small. Bordeaux, Bordeaux supérieur, Haut-Médoc, Médoc, Margaux, Pauillac, for instance, are all A.C. wines but Château Margaux, Château Lafite or any of the great wines need no official label of the kind.

Q. **Are any of the V.D.Q.S. wines deserving of the connoisseur's attention?**

[1] In 1962 the vineyards of France produced 73,478,000 hectolitres (1,616,516,000 gallons: 1,216,996,000 red and *rosés*; 399,520,000 white wines.

A. They are mostly regional wines made in small quantities, and of fair quality; many of them are certainly deserving of the connoisseur's attention.

Q. **Which French wines most interest the connoisseur?**
A. Above all, the wines of Bordeaux, Burgundy and Champagne, then the wines of Alsace, Arbois, the Loire, the Rhône, Provence and Roussillon.

Bordeaux

Q. **Where is Bordeaux?**
A. Bordeaux is on the left bank of the River Garonne, some 15 miles above the Bec d'Ambès, where Garonne and Dordogne meet and become La Gironde , a broad waterway to the Bay of Biscay.

Q. **What is Bordeaux?**
A. Bordeaux is, after Marseilles, the oldest port in France. The Romans occupied it some two thousand years ago and they were the first to praise its wines: ever since, ships laden with Bordeaux wine have sailed down the Gironde to all the ports of the world. Bordeaux is also one of the finest cities of France and the metropolis of the Gironde Department.

Q. **What is the Gironde Department?**
A. The Gironde Department is an administrative territorial unit which was carved, at the time of the French Revolution, out of ancient Guyenne and Gascony, south of the Cognac country, north of Bayonne and facing the Atlantic. Grapes grow practically everywhere in the Gironde Department, mostly in soil that is sandy, light and poor, yet richer than any of the world's gold mines: it has brought forth in the course of many centuries a wealth of wine beyond the dreams of avarice, and still shows no signs of exhaustion.

Q. **Are all the Gironde Department's wines Bordeaux wines?**
A. No wine is entitled to the name of Bordeaux wine which has been made from grapes grown outside the limits of the Gironde Department; but the wines of Gironde vineyards can only be marketed as

Bordeaux wines when their quality is up to the standard fixed by authority for the more homely or *ordinaires* wines sold as *Bordeaux rouges,* for the red wines, and *Bordeaux blancs,* for the white wines.

Q. **Which are the better Bordeaux wines?**
A. They are the wines sold as *Bordeaux supérieurs,* both red and white, but the whites may be sweet or dry. Then there are the wines which are sold under the name of their native village or district; their quality may not be superior to that of some *Bordeaux supérieurs* but they possess some degree of individuality which the others have not.

Q. **Which are the best wines of Bordeaux?**
A. They are the wines, be they red or white, which bear the name of their native vineyard or Château, whether the world-famous names of the great wines like Château Lafite and Château d'Yquem or the name of some little-known *bourgeois* vineyard producing wine that is not, of course, comparable with that of the great aristocrats yet possesses a highly respectable personality of its own which the wine connoisseur readily recognises.

Q. **Are the wines of Bordeaux the best of all French wines?**
A. There is no best wine other than the wine which you happen to like best: it is not only a matter of personal taste but of the mood of the moment. What entitles Bordeaux to the foremost place among the vinelands of the world is the fact that the vineyards of the Gironde Department still bring forth, as they have done for ages past, a greater quantity and a greater variety of quality wines than half all the other vineyards of the world put together, from 44 to 132 million gallons of wine in the worst and best of vintages.

Claret

Q. **What is Claret?**
A. Claret has been the name by which the red wines of Bordeaux have been known in England ever since the twelfth century.

Q. **Are any other red wines called Claret?**
A. Yes. Claret is not a geographical name like Sauternes or Chablis,

and there are other red beverage wines which look more or less like Claret and are called Claret, usually with the name of their country of origin added, as in Australian Claret and Spanish Claret.

Q. **Are all the Clarets from Bordeaux more or less alike?**

A. They are not, although they all have certain characteristics in common. Their colour, for instance, is never black nor pink; it is ruby, but there are a great many different shades and grades of ruby red in young and old Clarets, some of them similar or even identical to those of other red beverage wines. More specifically distinctive differences are those of the body, *bouquet* and breed of all Clarets. Body they all have, rough or smooth, stout or angular. *Bouquet*, that elusive perfume of flowers, is the privilege of the better wines after they have spent a while in bottle. Breed, as great a gift as it is rare, is the birthright of the aristocrats among wines.

Q. **Does not this apply to other wines besides Claret?**

A. Of course it does, but there are no other vinelands in the world with over four thousand named vineyards as there are in the Gironde Department, and even if half of them be written off as *ordinaires* there is still a unique range of wines to choose from, wines from fair to fine and from fine to great, a challenge to all wine connoisseurs and their joy.

Q. **Are there any different geographical categories of Clarets?**

A. There are five main geographical categories of Claret based on the two rivers Garonne and Dordogne, and the broad waterway called Gironde when those two meet and flow together into the Atlantic. On the left of the Gironde there is the Médoc, now divided into Haut Médoc, where most of the great Clarets come from, and Médoc, to seaward, where there is much wine made that is good but not great. On the right of the Gironde and in the islands of the Gironde, much Claret is made likewise, good but not great. On the left of the Garonne, from Barsac to Bordeaux, the Graves de Bordeaux vineyards produce much good and some great Claret, and the same may rightly be said of the much more extensive vineyards on the right of the Dordogne, chiefly those of St. Emilion and Pomerol. A great deal of Claret from middling to fair in quality is also made in the vineyards to the left of the Dordogne and the right

32

of the Garonne, a district known as Entre-deux-mers, literally 'Between two seas', instead of two rivers.

Q. **Are there any different categories of quality in Claret?**

A. Quality is a matter of personal appreciation but all good judges of Claret agree that there is no bad Claret: they also agree that Clarets made in the same locality and in the same year have every chance of being good, better and best according to the site of their native vineyard, because of its soil and subsoil, its aspect and altitude. Which is why in Bordeaux they may tell you that there are three main categories of quality in Clarets, the *Vins de Palus*, good wines, the *Vins de Côtes*, better wines, and the *Vins de Châteaux*, the best wines.

Q. **What are the Palus?**

A. They are the riverside vineyards. Their soil is mostly or partly of alluvial origin, deeper and richer than the soil of the hillsides and it brings forth a greater quantity of grapes per acre; but the wines made from *palus*-grown grapes, good as they may be in body, have little bouquet and no breed.

Q. **What are the Côtes?**

A. The *Côtes* are the hills where the soil is poorer, hence more suitable for quality wines. There are hills in many parts of the Gironde Department, chiefly on the right bank of the Garonne, many more above Libourne, from the Dordogne to the north-eastern boundaries of the Department, and the Blaye and Bourg country, on the right of the Gironde.

Q. **And where are the Châteaux?**

A. There are Châteaux everywhere, but the Châteaux of the Gironde are not showplaces like the Châteaux of the Loire. A few of them are very old and very interesting both architecturally and historically; most of them, however, are just the happy homes of the people who own the Château's vineyards and make the wine. Whether their Château be old or new, handsome or humble, makes no difference; it is a Château just as every Englishman's home is his castle.

Q. **Where are the Châteaux whose vineyards produce the best Clarets?**
They are in the Médoc, the Graves, St. Emilion and Pomerol.

33

Médoc

Q. **Where is the Médoc?**

A. The Médoc is a long strip of undulating country some 50 miles long from south to north and 5 miles wide, from the last 10 miles of the Garonne's run and the whole of the Gironde's 40 miles, on the east, to the barrage of sand dunes thrown up by the Atlantic, on the west. From the wine connoisseur's point of view, the Médoc should be divided into the Upper or Haut-Médoc, where most of the finest Clarets come from, and the Lower or Bas-Médoc.

Q. **Where is the Haut-Médoc?**

A. The Haut-Médoc is the name given to that part of the Médoc which lies from La Jalle de Blanquefort, a modest stream that flows into the Garonne, just below Bordeaux, to St. Seurin de Cadourne, some 35 miles farther north.

Q. **Which are the Châteaux of the Haut-Médoc whose vineyards produce the best Clarets?**

A. They are the sixty Châteaux which were graded or 'classified' officially, in 1855, in five groups of *crus classés*. It is generally admitted, however, that a number of the Châteaux placed in the lower groups over a hundred years ago now deserve a higher place.

Q. **In what part of the Haut-Médoc are the vineyards of the 60 Crus classes?**

A. Chiefly in the parishes of Margaux, Saint Julien, Pauillac and Saint Estèphe, and a few in six others of the parishes or *Communes* of the Haut-Médoc, i.e., Ludon, Macau, Labarde, Cantenac, Arsac, Saint Laurent.

Q. **Have any of the other vineyards and Châteaux of the Haut-Médoc been classified?**

A. Yes, hundreds of them have been classified according to the standard of excellence of their wines as *Crus exceptionnels, Crus Bourgeois Supérieurs, Crus Bourgeois* and *Crus Artisans*.

Q. **Which are the parishes or Communes of the Haut-Médoc which produce the best Clarets?**

34

A. Here is a list of those parishes of the Haut-Médoc from Blanque-fort, near Bordeaux, to the last *Commune* of the Haut-Médoc, with some particulars of their vinous output. (Tx. stands for *Tonneaux of red wine or Claret: a Tonneau holds 4 hogsheads, or about 100 dozen bottles of wine.* C.C. stands for *Crus classés*; C.E. for *Crus exceptionnels*; B.S. for *Crus Bourgeois Supérieurs*; B. for *Crus Bourgeois* and *Artisans*.)

BLANQUEFORT
   Château Tujean, B. 26 Tx (3 Tx white)
   Other B. Châteaux: 100 Tx (25 Tx white)
LE TAILLAN
   Château du Taillan: B. 20 Tx (20 Tx white 'La Dame Blanche')
   Château Fontanet: B. 30 Tx (5 Tx white)
   Other B. Châteaux: 55 Tx
SAINT AUBIN
   Château de Cujac: B. 5 Tx (2 Tx white)
   Other B. Châteaux: 100 Tx
SAINT MEDARD EN JALLE
   Château Vielleville: B. 15 Tx
   Other B. Châteaux: 34 Tx
PAREMPUYRE
   Château de Parempuyre: B. 35 Tx
   Château Ségur: B. 30 Tx
   Other B. Châteaux: 45 Tx (20 Tx white Clos Mon-Blanc)
LE PIAN MEDOC
   Moulin de Soubeyran: B. 10 Tx (5 Tx white)
   Château Sénéjac: B. 10 Tx
   Other B. Châteaux: 55 Tx
LUDON
   Château La Lagune: 3e C.C. 20 Tx
   Other Châteaux: B.S. 110 Tx;
                 B. 200 Tx (15 Tx white)
                 Palus, 600 Tx
MACAU
   Château Cantemerle: 5e C.C. 100 Tx., also 16 Tx of 'Second Vin' marketed as Royal Médoc.
   Other Châteaux: B.S. 240 Tx
                 B.200 Tx (15 Tx white)
                 Palus, 1,000 Tx

ARSAC, LABARDE and CANTENAC are three *Communes* nearest to the more important *Commune* of Margaux, and some of their vineyards are partly in the *Commune* of Margaux. Their wines are so similar to those of Margaux that they have been granted the right to be sold as Margaux wines. Their Châteaux and vinous output have also been included in the *Commune* of Margaux below.

MARGAUX

 Château Margaux: 1er C.C. 150 Tx (10 Tx white, Pavillon Blanc de Margaux)

 Château Rausan-Ségla: 2e C.C. 60 Tx

 Château Rauzan-Gassies: 2e C.C. 50 Tx

 Château Durfort: 2e C.C. 30 Tx

 Château Lascombes: 2e C.C. 50 Tx

 Château Brane-Cantenac: 2e C.C. 100 Tx

 Château Malescot-St. Exupéry: 3e C.C. 50 Tx

 Château Desmirail: 3e C.C. 30 Tx

 Château Ferrière: 3e C.C. 20 Tx

 Château Marquis d'Alesme-Becker: 3e C.C. 20 Tx

 Château Kirwan: 3e C.C. 100 Tx

 Château d'Issan: 3e C.C. 30 Tx

 Château Palmer: 3e C.C. 100 Tx

 Château Boyd-Cantenac: 3e C.C. 30 Tx

 Château Cantenac-Brown: 3e C.C. 90 Tx

 Château Giscours: 3e C.C. 20 Tx

 Château Marquis de Terme: 4e C.C. 75 Tx

 Château Pouget: 4e C.C. 30 Tx

 Château Le Prieuré Lichine: 4e C.C. 30 Tx

 Château Dauzac: 5e C.C. 60 Tx

 Château du Tertre: 5e C.C. 100 Tx

 Château Angludet: B.S. 100 Tx

 Château Montbrun: B.S. 25 Tx (10 Tx white wine marketed as Château Montbrun Goutte d'Or)

 Château d'Arsac: B.S. 20 Tx (10 Tx white)

 Château Monbrison: B.S. 10 Tx

 Château Siran: B.S. 100 Tx

AVENSAN

 Château Villegeorge: C.E. 20 Tx

 Château Citran: B.S. 60 Tx

 Other B.S. and B. Châteaux: 70 Tx

CASTELNAU
  B. 21 Tx
SOUSSANS
  Château Bel-Air Marquis d'Aligre: C.E. 30 Tx
  Château La Tour de Mons: B.S. 125 Tx
  Château Paveil de Luze: B.S. 20 Tx
  Other B.S. and B. 170 Tx
ARCINS
  B. 160 Tx
  Château Chasse-Spleen: C.E. 90 Tx
  21 other B.S. 700 Tx
LISTRAC
  Château Fonréaud: B.S. 100 Tx
  Château Lestage B.S. 125 Tx
  Château Clarke: B.S. 80 Tx (10 Tx white 'Clarke-Merle-Blanc')
  Château Sémeillan: B.S. 40 Tx
  Other B.S. 280 Tx
  Also Château La Mouette: 10 Tx white
LAMARQUE
  3 B.S. Châteaux: 75 Tx
  4 B. Châteaux: 50 Tx
CUSSAC
  Château Lanessan: B.S. 75 Tx
  3 other B.S. 100 Tx
  B. 500 Tx
SAINT-LAURENT
  Château La Tour Carnet: 4e C.C. 70 Tx
  Château Belgrave: 5e C.C. 150 Tx
  Château Camensac: 5e C.C. 70 Tx
  Château du Galan: B.S. 25 Tx
  3 other B.S. 120 Tx
  B. 500 Tx (also 100 Tx white)
SAINT-JULIEN
  Château Léoville Las Cases: 2e C.C. 150 Tx
  Château Léoville-Poyferré: 2e C.C. 120 Tx
  Château Léoville-Barton: 2e C.C. 100 Tx
  Château Gruaud-Larose: 2e C.C. 185 Tx
  Château Ducru Beaucaillou: 2e C.C. 130 Tx
  Château Langoa-Barton: 3e C.C. 75 Tx

Château Lagrange: 3e C.C. 100 Tx
Château St. Pierre Bontemps: 4e C.C. 40 Tx
Château St. Pierre Sevaistre: 4e C.C. 60 Tx
Château Branaire-Ducru: 4e C.C. 100 Tx
Château Talbot: 4e C.C. 140 Tx
Château Beychevelle: 4e C.C. 100 Tx
Château du Glana: B.S. 50 Tx
Château Moulin Riche: B.S. 30 Tx
Château Bontemps-Dubarry: B.S. 30 Tx
Château Sirène-Lafrange: 10 Tx white

PAUILLAC
Château Lafite-Rothschild: 1er C.C. 150 Tx
Château Latour: 1er C.C. 100 Tx
Château Mouton-Rothschild: 2e C.C. 75 Tx
Château Pichon-Longueville-Baron: 2e C.C. 78 Tx
Château Pichon-Longueville-Lalande: 2e C.C. 100 Tx
Château Duhart-Milon: 4e C.C. 140 Tx
Château Pontet-Canet: 5e C.C. 200 Tx
Château Batailley: 5e C.C. 80 Tx
Château Haut-Batailley: 5e C.C. 40 Tx
Château Grand-Puy-Ducasse: 5e C.C. 35 Tx
Château Lynch-Bages: 5e C.C. 100 Tx
Château Mouton Baron Philippe: 5e C.C. 100 Tx
Château Haut-Bages-Libéral: 5e C.C. 50 Tx
Château Pédesclaux: 5e C.C. 30 Tx
Château Clerc-Milon-Mondon: 5e C.C. 35 Tx
Château Croizet Bages: 5e C.C. 50 Tx
Château La Couronne: C.E. 15 Tx 19 B.S. 700 Tx

A number of B. produce about 1,000 Tx and some of their wines are handled by the *Cooperative des Propriétaires de Pauillac* and marketed as '*Grand Vin La Rose Pauillac*'.

SAINT SAUVEUR
3 B.S. 165 Tx
B. 300 Tx

CISSAC
Château Hauteillan: B. 150 Tx
Château Cissac: B. 30 Tx
Other B. Châteaux: 285 Tx

SAINT ESTEPHE

Château Cos d'Estournel: 2ᵉ C.C. 50 Tx
Château Montrose: 2ᵉ C.C. 100 Tx
Château Calon-Ségur: 3ᵉ C.C. 150 Tx
Château Cos Labory: 5ᵉ C.C. 45 Tx
Château Meyney: B.S. 150 Tx
Château Le Crock: B.S. 125 Tx
Château de Marbuzet: B.S. 50 Tx
Château Beau-Site: B.S. 100 Tx
Château Phèlan-Ségur: B.S. 150 Tx
Château Capbern: B.S. 90 Tx
Château Grand-Village-Capbern: B.S. 30 Tx
Château La Rose Capbern: B.S. 20 Tx

22 other B.S. produce another 1,000 Tx and the Cooperative of St. Estèphe deals with the wines of some 140 small *vignerons* producing an average of 140 Tx of B. wines.

There are two more *Communes* in the Haut Médoc—Vertheuil and Saint Seurin de Cadourne—before the Lower or Bas Médoc, now called Médoc.

Q. **Which are the Communes of the Bas Médoc or Médoc?**

A. There are 21 *Communes* in the Médoc from St. Seurin de Cadourne to Soulac by the Bay of Biscay. Their vineyards produce on an average 16,700 *tonneaux* of wine, mostly red and mostly of the *ordinaires* class. Among the Châteaux of the Médoc where greater skill and care in the cultivation of the vineyards and the making of the wine are responsible for a higher standard of quality, mention should be made of the following:

Château du Castéra: 125 Tx (125 Tx white)
Château Laujac: 150 Tx
Château Loudenne: 100 Tx
Château Livran: 125 Tx (50 Tx white)

Bourg and Blaye

Q. **Is there as much wine made upon the right bank of the Gironde as there is on the left?**

A. There is a great deal more. All the vineyards of both the Haut-

39

Médoc and the Médoc do not produce more than 45,000 *tonneaux* of red wine and 1,500 *tonneaux* of white per annum, a total of 46,500 *tonneaux*, but the total yield of the vineyards of the Bourgeais and Blayais, on the opposite or right side of the Gironde, adds up to 36,500 *tonneaux* of red wine and 36,500 *tonneaux* of white, a total of 73,000 *tonneaux*.

Q. **Which are the more important estates of the Bourgeais?**
A. They are:

    Château du Bousquet: 150 Tx
    Château de la Grave: 150 Tx and 40 Tx white
    Château Mille Secousses: 250 Tx
    Château Eyquem: 100 Tx and 15 Tx white
    Château de Barbe: 200 Tx
    Château Grand Jour: 125 Tx and 15 Tx white

Q. **Which are the more important estates of the Blayais?**
A. They are:

    Château Gontier: 100 Tx
    Château Bellevue: 80 Tx
    Domaine de Saint Germain: 60 Tx and 20 Tx white
    Château Pardaillan: 75 Tx
    Château Crusquet: 100 Tx
    Château Lescadre: 150 Tx
    Château Cazeaux: 100 Tx and 60 Tx white
    Château Le Menaudat: 50 Tx and 20 Tx white
    Château La Pitance: 100 Tx and 100 Tx white
    Château Virou: 300 Tx and 50 Tx white.

Graves, red and white

Q. **Where is the Graves district?**
A. The Graves or, to be more precise, the Graves de Bordeaux, as there are some vineyards with similar gravelly soil known as Graves de St. Emilion, is a stretch of well-wooded country with great and small patches of vineyards here and there, along the left bank of the River Garonne for approximately 25 miles from Bordeaux southwards.

Q. **Is the Graves de Bordeaux country much smaller than the Médoc?**

A. It is much smaller but its vineyards can claim greater antiquity: some of them were flourishing in Roman and Medieval times.

Q. **Are there any Châteaux in the Graves country?**

A. There are not so many Châteaux of Graves as there are in the Médoc, but there are some of great beauty and historical interest.

Q. **Have the Graves vineyards ever been officially classified?**

A. They have not been officially classified, with the exception of Château Haut-Brion which was given, in 1855, a place alongside the three *Premiers crus classés* of the Médoc; Lafite, Latour and Margaux.

Q. **Are not Graves wines mostly white wines?**

A. No, there are on an average 6,000 Tx of white Graves to 9,000 Tx of red Graves, but as the white wines are marketed under the name of Graves and the red wines as Claret, it is popularly accepted that 'Graves' means a white Bordeaux.

Q. **Are the white wines of Graves as good as the red, or better?**

A. The majority of white Graves wines are sold as 'Graves' or 'Graves supérieures', or under the registered name or brand of wine merchants; they are mostly *ordinaires* wines. The better white wines of Graves which are sold under the name of their native Château are good or very good table wines, but none of them can rightly claim to be great, whereas there are some great red Graves – the peers of the great wines of the Médoc; and there are, of course, many more red than white Graves in the good and very good categories. The exceptions to this general rule are very few, and Haut Brion Blanc is perhaps the only one.

Q. **How do the red wines of Graves differ from those of the Médoc?**

A. The Graves Clarets are on the whole softer and possess a more obvious or understandable charm. The Médocs are firmer, more standoffish, but they possess more breed. In colour and alcoholic strength they are alike but they all have a *bouquet* of their own. No connoisseur, for instance, could fail to recognise the *bouquet* of a Château Margaux and the *bouquet* of a Château Haut-Brion: they are as different as the perfume of violets and that of wallflowers.

41

Q. **Which are the Châteaux whose vineyards produce the best Graves wines, red and white?**

A. They are the following châteaux, not in order of merit but according to their *Communes* or parishes from Bordeaux southwards and westwards:

PESSAC

 Château Haut-Brion: 1er C.C. 100 Tx red

 Château La Mission Haut-Brion: 45 Tx red

 Château Pape Clément: 50 Tx red

 Château Fanning-La-Fontaine: 30 Tx red

TALENCE

 Château La Tour Haut-Brion: 15 Tx red

VILLENAVE D'ORNON

 Château Baret: 80 Tx red; 25 Tx white

 Château Couhins: 15 Tx red; 40 Tx white

 Château Cantebau-Couhins: 15 Tx white

GRADIGNAN

 Château Moulerens: 20 Tx red

 Château Poumey: 20 Tx red

LEOGNAN

 Château Haut-Bailly: 30 Tx red

 Château La Louvière: 85 Tx red

 Château Malartic-La-Gravière: 30 Tx red

 Château Carbonnieux: 60 Tx red; 80 Tx white

 Château Olivier: 20 Tx red: 100 Tx white

 Domaine de Chevalier: 30 Tx red

 Château Chevalier: 4 Tx white

 Château Le Pape: 25 Tx red; 5 Tx white

 Château Brown: 40 Tx red; 60 Tx white

 Château Larrivet-Haut-Brion: 20 Tx red

 Château Fieuzal: 30 Tx red; 15 Tx white

MARTILLAC

 Château Smith-Haut-Lafitte: 50 Tx red

 Château La Garde: 100 Tx red

 Château La Tour Martillac et Kressmann: 10 Tx red; 15 Tx white

BEGLES

 Château de Hilde: 30 Tx red

CADAUJAC

 Château Bouscaut: 100 Tx red; 50 Tx white

BEAUTIRAN
   Château le Tuquet: 160 Tx red
CASTRES
   Château Ferrande: 10 Tx red; 6 Tx white
LA BREDE
   Château de La Brède: 16 Tx white

Sauternes

Q. **What about Sauternes?**

A. Sauternes is the name of a village some 3 miles west of Langon, which is about 30 miles south of Bordeaux on the left bank of the Garonne. Sauternes is a small place but it has given its name to one of the great white wines of the world.

Q. **Do all Sauternes wines come from the vineyards of Sauternes?**

A. No. All genuine Sauternes come from what is known as the Sauternes country, a stretch of land which is practically the continuation of the Graves country, along the left bank of the Garonne from the valley of the little river Ciron, which flows into the Garonne at Barsac, up to a little beyond Langon. There are four *Communes*, besides the Sauternes *Communes*, whose wines are entitled to the name of Sauternes.

Q. **Which are those Communes?**

A. They are the four which adjoin Sauternes north, south, east and west – Bommes, Barsac, Preignac and Fargues.

Q. **Are there not other white wines called Sauternes?**

A. There are a number of white wines, white and sweet, which have been given the name of Sauternes because of the prestige attached to the name even though they have no right to it. As a rule these false Sauternes drop the final 's' and call themselves Sauterne.

Q. **Is Sauternes sweetened?**

A. No. Sauternes is a sweet wine but not a sweetened wine. It is sweet because it is made from over-ripe white grapes so rich in grape sugar that fermentation cannot use it all.

43

Q. **Are all Sauternes more or less alike?**

A. There is a family likeness which belongs to the wines of the five Sauternes *Communes* as well as to their cousins—the white wines made from the same species of grapes and in the same manner nearby on both the left and the right banks of the Garonne; but there are, of course, different grades of quality.

Q. **Are there any Sauternes Châteaux?**

A. Yes, there are a number of Sauternes Châteaux and they were classified in 1885, at the same time as the Châteaux of the Médoc.

Q. **Which are the classified Châteaux of Sauternes?**

A. Château d'Yquem stands in a class by itself as the finest of them all. The Château itself stands fortress-like upon a knoll about a mile from the village of Sauternes, surrounded by its 220 acres of vine-yards which produce one of the greatest of the sweet white wines of the world—not great because it is sweet but because of its *bouquet* and breed and also of its power to stand the test of age. It is one of the very few white wines which improve with age.

Q. **Which are the other classified Châteaux of Sauternes?**

A. They are, according to their *Communes,* the following:
SAUTERNES
 Château Guiraud: 1er C.C. 80 Tx
 Château Filhot: 2^e C.C. 50 Tx
 Château d'Arche: 2^e C.C. 12 Tx
 Château d'Arche Lafaurie: 2^e C.C. 14 Tx
 Château d'Arche Vimeney: 2^e C.C. 12 Tx
 Château Lamothe: 2^e C.C. 10 Tx
 Château Lamothe-Bergey: 2^e C.C. 20 Tx
 Château Raymond-Lafon: 2^e C.C. 35 Tx
BOMMES
 Château La Tour Blanche: 1er C.C. 65 Tx
 Château Lafaurie-Peyraguey: 1er C.C. 45 Tx
 Château Rayne-Vigneau: 1er C.C. 75 Tx
 Château Rabaud: 1er C.C. 60 Tx
 Clos Haut-Peyraguey: 1er C.C. 15 Tx
BARSAC
 Château Coutet: 1er C.C. 60 Tx

44

Château Climens: 1er C.C. 45 Tx
Château Doisy-Védrines: 2e C.C. 40 Tx
Château Doisy-Daëne: 2e C.C. 12 Tx
Château Doisy-Dubroca: 2e C.C. 15 Tx
Château Myrat: 2e C.C. 40 Tx
Château Broustet: 2e C.C. 30 Tx
Château Caillou: 2e C.C. 40 Tx
Château Suau: 2e C.C. 15 Tx
Château Nairac: 2e C.C. 30 Tx

PREIGNAC
Château Suduiraut: 1er C.C. 100 Tx
Château de Malle: 2^e C.C. 40 Tx

FARGUES
Château Rieussec: 1er C.C. 70 Tx
Château Romer: 2^e C.C. 15 Tx

Q. **Are there any 'Crus Bourgeois' of Sauternes?**
A. There are many, chiefly in the *Commune* of Barsac. They are just as sweet as the others but they have not got either their *finesse* or their distinction.

Q. **Are they much cheaper?**
A. No, they are never really cheap.

Q. **Are there no cheap Sauternes?**
A. No, there are no cheap Sauternes, but there are many sweet white wines of the near-Sauternes type which are much cheaper and yet still very sweet.

Q. **How are the cheaper types of Sauternes marketed?**
A. Some, which are blends of genuine white wines of the lesser vineyards of the Sauternes country, are marketed as either 'Sauternes' or 'Barsac', without the name of a particular vineyard and without the date of a vintage; some, which are a little dearer and are supposed to be a little better, are dubbed 'Haut-Sauternes' or 'Haut-Barsac'; some are blends marketed under the name, or brand, of the shippers or merchants; some, and they are probably better value, are the white wines of Cérons, Ste. Croix du Mont, and the Premières Côtes de Bordeaux.

Q. **Where is Cérons?**

A. Cérons is on the left bank of the Garonne at the southern end of the Graves de Bordeaux country, next to the Sauternais.

Q. **Where is Ste. Croix du Mont?**

A. Ste. Croix du Mont is on the right bank of the Garonne, almost facing Langon.

Q. **Where are the Premières Côtes de Bordeaux?**

A. They are the vineyards on the right bank of the Garonne from Bordeaux to Langon. They produce a very large quantity of wine, well over 3 million gallons on an average every year.

Q. **Are the Premières Côtes de Bordeaux wines red or white?**

A. They produce both. From Bordeaux to Cambes they produce more red wines than white; but then, on to Langon, they produce a very much greater proportion of white wine than red.

Q. **Are the Premières Côtes wines *ordinaires* or quality wines?**

A. Most of them are of the *ordinaires* class, but there are some notable exceptions among the white wines, such as the wines of Château Ricaud (Loupiac), and Château de Tastes (Ste. Croix du Mont).

Q. **Are there any Deuxièmes Côtes de Bordeaux?**

A. Not by that name, but there are vineyards upon the hills which are virtually a continuation of the Premières Côtes de Bordeaux alongside the Garonne, to the south; they are known as Côtes de Bordeaux St. Macaire and they produce some 3,500 Tx of red wines and 5,500 Tx of white wines per annum.

Q. **Which have been the best 20th century vintages for Sauternes?**

A. 1900, 1901, 1904, 1908, 1914, 1919, 1921, 1926, 1928, 1929, 1934, 1937, 1942, 1943, 1945, 1947, 1948, 1949, 1953, 1955, 1957, 1959.

Entre-Deux-Mers

Q. **What is the meaning of Entre-Deux-Mers?**

A. It means the land – its fields, pastures, woods and, of course, its vineyards–that lies between the Garonne and the Dordogne above Bordeaux, in the Gironde Department.

Q. **Are there many vineyards in the Entre-Deux-Mers?**
A. There must be a great many vineyards since the official statistics give the total yearly average quantity of wine made from Entre-Deux-Mers vineyards as 26,000 *tonneaux* of red wines and 50,000 of white wines.

Q. **Are any of the Entre-Deux-Mers wines quality wines?**
A. No, they are wines for the thirsty–and there are many of them–but not for the connoisseurs, of whom there are not so many. All the better white Entre-Deux-Mers wines, however, have their own *Appellation contrôlée*.

Saint Emilion, Pomerol

Q. **What about St. Emilion?**
A. St. Emilion is a very ancient city perched upon one of the hills above Libourne well back from the right bank of the Dordogne. St. Emilion is surrounded by a billowing sea of vineyards, up hill and down dale, as far as the eye can see, and most of their wines are entitled to the name of St. Emilion.

Q. **Are there any St. Emilion Châteaux?**
A. There are a great many, some of them close to the city, others lower down the hill and yet others in different parts of the St. Emilion *Commune* and in a score of other nearby *Communes*.

Q. **Are the St. Emilion Châteaux classified like the Châteaux of the Médoc?**
A. They were not classified like the Châteaux of the Médoc, in 1855, but there was a classification made in 1955, when Château Ausone (25 Tx) and Château Cheval Blanc (100 Tx) were placed in Class A, ahead of all others; 9 others in Class B; and 65 more were named as *Grands Crus classés*. The Class B. Châteaux are, in alphabetical order:

Château Beauséjour: 45 Tx

Château Belair: 40 Tx
Château Canon: 75 Tx
Clos Fourtet: 50 Tx
Château Figeac: 100 Tx
Château La Gaffelière-Naudes: 80 Tx
Château Magdelaine: 20 Tx
Château Pavie: 150 Tx
Château Trottevieille: 30 Tx

Grands Crus classés:

Clos de l'Angelus: 100 Tx
L'Arrosée: 20 Tx
Balestard-la-Tonnelle: 30 Tx
Bellevue: 30 Tx
Bergat: 15 Tx
Berliquet: 35 Tx
Cadet-Bon: 30 Tx
Cadet-Piola: 15 Tx
Canon-la-Gaffelière: 40 Tx
Cap-de-Mourlin: 50 Tx
Chauvin: 35 Tx
Corbin: 50 Tx
Corbin-Michotte: 50 Tx
Croque-Michotte: 40 Tx
Coutet: 40 Tx
Curé-Bon-La-Madeleine: 12 Tx
Faurie-de-Soutard: 50 Tx
Fonplégade: 35 Tx
Fonroque: 80 Tx
Franc-Mayne: 30 Tx
Grand-Barrail-Lamarzelle: 100 Tx
Grand Corbin-Despagne: 60 Tx
Grand Corbin-David: 25 Tx
Domaine du Grand Faure: 20 Tx
Grand Mayne: 60 Tx
Grand Pontet: 25 Tx
Grandes Murailles: 25 Tx
Guadet-Saint-Julien: 30 Tx
Jean Faure: 30 Tx
Haut Simard: 30 Tx

Clos des Jacobins: 40 Tx
La Carte: 15 Tx
La Clotte: 16 Tx
La Cluzière: 12 Tx
La Couspaude: 40 Tx
La Dominique: 40 Tx
Clos La Madeleine: 6 Tx
Larcis-Ducasse: 40 Tx
Lamarzelle: 25 Tx
Larmande: 25 Tx
Laroze: 100 Tx
La Serre: 20 Tx
La Tour-du-Pin-Figeac-Moueix: 50 Tx
La Tour-Figeac: 60 Tx
Le Châtelet: 12 Tx
Le Couvent: 60 Tx
Le Prieuré-St. Emilion: 10 Tx
Mauvezin: 7 Tx
Moulin-du-Cadet: 10 Tx
Pavie-Decesse: 25 Tx
Pavie-Macquin: 60 Tx
Pavillon-Cadet: 20 Tx
Petit-Faurie-de-Soutard: 40 Tx
Petit-Faurie-de-Souchard: 40 Tx
Ripeau: 40 Tx
Sansonnet: 40 Tx
Saint-Georges-Côte-Pavie: 20 Tx
Clos Saint-Martin: 6 Tx
Soutard: 60 Tx
Tertre-Daugay: 30 Tx
Trimoulet: 25 Tx
Trois-Moulins: 15 Tx
Troplong-Mondot: 120 Tx
Villemaurine: 25 Tx
Yon-Figeac: 75 Tx
Monbousquet: 75 Tx–St. Emilionnais, not in the List but a good wine.

The average annual production of the vineyards of St. Emilion is 6,300 Tx and that of nearby vineyards entitled to sell their wines as

St. Emilion 8,250 Tx, with a further 10,450 Tx of wines of the St. Emilionnais or St. Emilion district, a grand total of 43,000 Tx of red wines mostly of honest-to-God quality, stoutish, homely and ready to drink quite young, hence also cheaper than most Bordeaux wines.

Q. **What about Pomerol?**

A. Pomerol is a small plateau between Libourne and St. Emilion with about 1,800 acres of vineyards: they produce on an average 1,500 Tx of Claret of very good quality, and a further 1,000 Tx of more *ordinaires* wines.

Q. **Which are the best wines of Pomerol?**

A. The best wine of Pomerol is that of Château Petrus (35 Tx) which its late owner, Madame Loubat, always refused to sell at any price below that of the First Growths of the Médoc of the same vintages. There are, besides, some fifty Châteaux, mostly with very small vineyards, which rank as *Grands Crus*. The following are among the more important and better known in England:

Beauregard: 35 Tx
Certan: 10 Tx
Gazin: 80 Tx
La Fleur Petrus: 20 Tx
La Pointe: 70 Tx
La Tour Pomerol: 40 Tx
Trotanoy: 25 Tx
La Conseillante: 40 Tx
L'Evangile: 45 Tx
Nénin: 100 Tx
Petit Village: 40 Tx
Plince: 100 Tx
de Sales: 100 Tx
Vieux Château Certan: 40 Tx

Q. **What is Lalande de Pomerol?**

A. It is the name of the *Commune* immediately to the north of Pomerol, next to the *Commune* of Néac, to the north-east of Pomerol. The vineyards of both Néac and Lalande de Pomerol produce some 2,000 *tonneaux* of red wines, from *ordinaires* to fair in quality, comparable with the wines of the *Bourgeois* and *Artisans* growths of Pomerol.

Q. **Where is Fronsac?**

A. Fronsac and the Fronsadais or Fronsac country is more to the west: it rises from the right bank of the Dordogne and of its tributary l'Isle to the highlands in the north of the Gironde Department. Its vineyards produce some 20,000 *tonneaux* of red wine per annum and some 2,000 *tonneaux* of white wine from *ordinaires* to fair in quality. The showplace of the Fronsadais is Château Rouet, in the *Commune* of St. Germain la Rivière. Its vineyards produce some 125 *tonneaux* of red wine and the view from its terrace over the Dordogne Valley and beyond is the finest there is in the Gironde.

Q. **What is the meaning of 'Château bottled'?**

A. A Château-bottled Claret is a wine which has been bottled at its native vineyard by the staff of its native Château. It bears on its label the words '*Mis en bouteilles au Château*' or '*Mise en bouteilles du Château*'; its name and vintage are also stamped on its cork.

Q. **Is a Château-bottled Claret better than the wine of the same vintage bottled in England?**

A. It is bound to be a dearer wine but not necessarily a better wine. It costs more because the duty on wine imported in bottles is higher than the duty on the same wine imported in casks, but a Claret can be, and has been, bottled in London and Leith, Bristol and Liverpool with greater care and skill, born of greater experience, than at some of the Bordeaux châteaux where the staff's chief business is to grow grapes and to make wine, not to bottle it. Château bottling's chief virtue from the customer's point of view is that it is a certificate of origin, even if no longer a certificate of quality as it was when Château bottling was reserved for wines of the best vintages.

Q. **Which are the best Claret vintages of the twentieth century?**

A. 1900, 1905, 1906, 1908, 1911, 1916, 1920, 1921, 1924, 1926, 1928, 1929, 1934, 1937, 1945, 1947, 1949, 1953, 1955, 1959, 1961.

Dordogne

Q. **Are the wines of the Dordogne Bordeaux wines?**

A. The wines known as Dordogne wines are those which are made from grapes grown in the Dordogne Department. Wines made from grapes grown on the right of the River Dordogne, in the St. Emilion region, or on the left, in the Entre-Deux-Mers region, within the boundaries of the Gironde Department, are Bordeaux wines, and classified accordingly.

Q. **Where is the Dordogne Department?**

A. The Dordogne Department lies immediately east of the Gironde and west of the Creuse; the Dordogne river runs through it; there are vineyards in many parts on both sides of the Dordogne river: they add up to 90,000 acres; they have an optimum production of 22 million gallons of wine, 45% white wines, and 35% A.C. or quality wines.

Q. **Which are the best wines of the Dordogne?**

A. They are the sweet white wines of Monbazillac.

Q. **Which are the next best wines of the Dordogne?**

A. They are the wines of the Montravel region, a continuation of the Entre-deux-Mers region of the Gironde Department.

Q. **What are Vins de Maccadam?**

A. *Vins de Maccadam* is the name given locally to some sweetish white wines of the Montravel region, which are inexpensive and pleasant to drink when very young, but not later.

Q. **Which are the best red wines of the Dordogne?**

A. They are the Pécharmants from vineyards north of Bergerac. They have their own *Appellation contrôlée* and so have Bergerac, Monbazillac and Montravel.

Burgundy

Q. **What is Burgundy?**

A. Burgundy is the English name of both *La Bourgogne* and *Le Bourgogne*. La Bourgogne is the name of one of the greatest of the old Provinces of France, now divided into smaller Departments, chiefly the *Yonne,* the *Côte d'Or* and the *Saône-et-Loire.* Le Bourgogne is the name of the wine made from grapes of the vineyards of La Bourgogne.

Q. **Are there many wines called Burgundy which are not made in Burgundy?**

A. There are a number of wines, more particularly red wines, made in Spain, Australia, California and elsewhere which look like Burgundy and are made to taste somewhat like Burgundy: they are marketed as Spanish Burgundy, Australian Burgundy, California Burgundy and so on, in the United Kingdom, where the name 'Burgundy' is not protected by the law of the land, like Port, Madeira, and Champagne; also in the U.S.A. where the European geographical names of wine are not protected by law.

Q. **Which types of wine are made from grapes grown in Burgundy?**

A. The genuine wines of Burgundy are mostly table and beverage wines, either red or white. Most genuine Burgundy wines are very pleasant but undistinguished. Being made from the Gamay grape (red wines), or the Aligoté (white wines), both white and red wines enjoy the privilege of being most acceptable when quite young. There is also a very important quantity of exceptionally fine wines made in Burgundy, the peers of the greatest wines of the world: the red wines are made from Pinot Noir grapes and the whites from Pinot Chardonnay from vineyards of the Yonne and Côte d'Or departments only.

Q. **Do they not make in Burgundy a wine which they call Passe-tous-grains?**

A. Passetoutgrain or Passe-tous-grains is a red Burgundy made from both Gamay and Pinot grapes, or from the last bunches of grapes to be picked at the time of the vintage. They are not fine wines, but they may be of fair quality and better value than other *ordinaires* wines.

Q. **Are the wines of Burgundy quite different from the wines of Bordeaux?**

A. Yes, they are. The white wines of Burgundy are not only much drier but they possess a distinctive charm and appeal that is entirely their own. Red Burgundy often has a deeper shade of red than

Claret, a more developed or obvious *bouquet* and a slightly higher alcoholic strength, but there is a more subtle difference between red Burgundy and Claret: it is one of flavour or 'tone': it might be compared to the difference between soprano (Bordeaux) and contralto (Burgundy). When both are of the same quality, there cannot be any question of one being better than the other.

Q. **What is the cause of the difference between Burgundy and Bordeaux?**

A. There are various causes but the chief one is that the grapes from which the wines are made are different. All the best wines of Burgundy, both red and white, are made from the one species of grapes known as Pinots, whilst all the good Clarets are made from a trinity of grapes, mostly Cabernets, Malbecs and Merlots, and all the better Bordeaux white wines are made from Sauvignon-Semillon. All these different species of grapes have been chosen as the best suited to the entirely different soil and climate of west (Bordeaux) and east (Burgundy). There are also the local techniques of wine-making which are not the same in Bordeaux and in Burgundy.

Q. **Are the wines of Burgundy more lasting than those of Bordeaux?**

A. No, they are not. They mature more rapidly and are, as a rule, ready to drink at an earlier age, but all the great Clarets and Sauternes stand the test of time – that is, improve with age – better than Burgundies, red or white.

Q. **Do the vineyards of Burgundy produce a greater quantity of wine than those of Bordeaux?**

A. No, they do not. The Gironde Department produces a great deal more wine than the four Departments of Burgundy.

Q. **Which are the Departments which produce Burgundy?**

A. They are the Côte d'Or, with 22,000 acres; the Saône-et-Loire, with 35,000 acres; the Rhône, with 50,000 acres; and the Yonne, with 10,000 acres of vineyards.

Q. **Which are the best vineyards of the Côte d'Or?**

A. They are the vineyards upon the lower slopes of two groups of hills on the right of the Route Nationale No. 74, from Dijon to Lyons for some 30 miles before Santenay, where the Côte d'Or ends, and Chagny, where the Saône-et-Loire begins. The first group of hills is called Côte de Nuits and the other Côte de Beaune, and their vineyards, planted in noble Pinots, produce all the quality wines. On the left of the Route Nationale there are many more vineyards, planted with the common Gamay grape, in the undulating lowlands rolling eastwards towards the Saône, but their wines are *ordinaires*: they bring forth on an average 50% of the total Côte d'Or wines.

Q. **Which are the vineyards which produce the finest Burgundies?**
A. The vineyards of the Côte de Nuits, from Fixin, about 4 miles south of Dijon, to Corgoloin, about the same distance north of Beaune, about 3,000 acres in all. They produce the greatest of all red Burgundies as well as a small quantity of fine white wines. Also the vineyards of the Côte de Beaune, from Aloxe-Corton to Santenay, about 6,000 acres in all; they produce a greater quantity of red wines, mostly very good wines indeed, but very few of them equal in *finesse* or breed to the best red wines of the Côte de Nuits. On the other hand, they are responsible for a greater quantity of white wines, and most of them are the finest white wines of Burgundy.

Côte de Nuits

Q. **Which are the best vineyards of the Côte de Nuits?**
A. They are, in geographical order, from north to south, in the *Communes* or parishes of Fixin, Gevrey-Chambertin, Morey-St.-Denis, Chambolle-Musigny, Vougeot, Flagey-Echézeaux, Vosne-Romanée, and Nuits-St.-Georges. All red wines sold under the name of any of those *Communes* are good wines but the better wines always bear the names of their native vineyards.

Q. **Which is the best vineyard of Fixin?**
A. La Perrière (12 acres).

Q. **Which are the best vineyards of Gevrey-Chambertin?**
A. Le Chambertin (32·5 acres)
Clos de Bèze (37·5 acres)
Latricières-Chambertin (17·5 acres)

Charmes-Chambertin (31 acres)
Mazys-Chambertin (21·5 acres)
Ruchottes-Chambertin (8·5 acres)
Chapelle-Chambertin (20 acres)
Griotte-Chambertin (7·5 acres)
Mazoyères-Chambertin (37·5 acres)
Clos St. Jacques (17·5 acres)

Q. **Which are the best vineyards of Morey-Saint-Denis?**
A. Clos de Tart (17·5 acres)
Bonnes Mares, part of (5 acres)
Clos des Lambrays (22 acres)
Clos de la Roche (11 acres)
Clos Saint-Denis (5 acres)

Q. **Which are the best vineyards of Chambolle Musigny?**
A. Bonnes Mares, part of (5 acres)
Les Musigny (25 acres)
Les Amoureuses (13·5 acres)

Q. **Which is the best vineyard of Vougeot?**
A. Le Clos de Vougeot, the best and largest with 125 acres shared by 54 different owners. There is also in the *Commune* of Vougeot a small white grapes vineyard known as Le Clos Blanc.

Q. **Which are the best vineyards of Flagey-Echézeaux?**
A. Les Grands Echézeaux (23 acres)
Les Echézeaux (10·6 acres)

Q. **Which are the best vineyards of Vosne Romanée?**
A. Romanée Conti (4·5 acres)
La Romanée (2 acres)
La Tâche (14·5 acres)
Les Richebourg (20 acres)
Romanée Saint-Vivant (24 acres)

Q. **Is Romanée Conti the only vineyard in Burgundy with pre-Phylloxera vines?**
A. Romanée Conti kept its *vieilles vignes* for a very long time but they

had to be done away with in 1945. There was but very little wine made in that year, and none at all from 1946 to 1951, as the replanted vines did not come into bearing before 1952.

Q. **Which are the best vineyards of Nuits-Saint-Georges?**
A. Le Saint-Georges (19 acres)
Les Porrets (17·5 acres)
Les Vaucrains (15 acres)
Les Boudots (16 acres)
Les Cailles (10 acres)
Les Pruliers (17·5 acres)

Q. **Which are the best vineyards of Prémeaux?**
A. Clos de la Maréchale (24 acres)
Les Corvées (20 acres)
Clos Arlot (18·5 acres)

Q. **Do all these vineyards produce red wine?**
A. They do, but there are a few vineyards in the Côte de Nuits where they grow white grapes and make a little white wine: the best is the Musigny Blanc, and the next best the wine of the Clos Blanc de Vougeot. What white wine is made at Morey Saint-Denis and elsewhere is of fair but not remarkable quality.

Côte de Beaune

Q. **Which are the best wines of the Côte de Beaune?**
A. They are the wines of the best vineyards of the *Communes* of Aloxe-Corton, Ladoix-Serrigny, Pernand-Vergelesses, Savigny-les-Beaune, Beaune, Pommard, Volnay, Monthélie, Auxey-Duresse, Meursault, Puligny-Montrachet, Chassagne-Montrachet and Santenay.

Q. **Which are the best vineyards of Aloxe-Corton?**
A. Le Corton (28 acres) mostly red wine
Le Clos du Roi (26 acres) all red wine
En Charlemagne (42·5 acres) mostly white wine
Les Chaumes (5·5 acres) all red wine
Les Renardes (32·5 acres) all red wine

These are the only five *Têtes de Cuvée* but some of the *Premières Cuvées*, such as Les Bressandes (42·5 acres) and La Vigne-au-Saint (6·5 acres), produce some very fine red wines. There are also other *Premières Cuvées* where white wine is made as well as red (Les Pougets; Les Longuettes).

Q. **Is Corton-Grancey the wine of a Corton *Tête de Cuvée* or *Première Cuvée*?**

A. Corton-Grancey is the registered name of a very fine wine marketed by the firm of Louis Latour. It is made from grapes grown in their own vineyards, in the *Commune* of Aloxe-Corton.

Q. **Is there no worth while vineyard in the Commune of Ladoix-Serrigny?**

A. Yes, there is Le Clos des Cortons Faiveley (25 acres) which ranks as a *Première Cuvée;* its vineyard adjoins those of Aloxe-Corton and the wine is sold as a Corton.

Q. **Which is the best vineyard of Pernand-Vergelesses?**
A. Ile de Vergelesses (23 acres)

Q. **Which are the best vineyards of Savigny-les-Beaune?**
A. Les Vergelesses (42 acres)
Les Marconnets (23 acres)
Les Jarrons (22·5 acres)

Q. **Which are the best vineyards of Beaune?**
A. Les Fèves (11 acres)
Les Grèves (79·5 acres)
Les Marconnets (25·5 acres)
Les Bressandes (46 acres)
Les Cras (12 acres)
Les Champimonts (41·5 acres)
Le Clos de la Mousse (8·5 acres)
Le Clos-des-Mouches (62 acres) some white wine as well as red.

Q. **What about the Hospices de Beaune Burgundies?**
A. The Hospices de Beaune is a group of hospitals. The oldest of them, the Hôtel-Dieu, was built in the fifteenth century by Chancelier

Nicolas Rolin and his wife Guigone de Salins. They bequeathed to their foundation, as an endowment, all the vineyards which they owned at the time; other well-wishers have done the same in the course of the past five centuries. Every year the wines made from the vineyards which now belong to the Hospices de Beaune are sold by public auction on the third Sunday of November – not under the name of any particular vineyard but under the name of the donor of the vineyard or that of some benefactor, so that all genuine Hospices de Beaune Burgundies bear the name of one or the other of the following *Cuvées* identified with the Hospices benefactors: also the names of the *Communes* of the vineyards.

RED WINES

Communes and Cuvées
ALOXE-CORTON
  Dr Peste
  Charlotte Dumay
SAVIGNY-LES-BEAUNE
  Fouquerand
  Du Bay-Peste
  Cyrot
  Forneret
BEAUNE
  Dames Hospitalières
  Guigone de Salins
  Rousseau-Deslandes
  Brunet
  Nicolas Rolin
  Betault
  Estienne
POMMARD
  Dames de la Charité
  Billardet
VOLNAY
  Blondeau
MONTHELIE
  Lebelin
  Henri Gélicot

AUXEY-DURESSE
Boillot

WHITE WINES

MEURSAULT
Jehan de Massol
Gauvain
De Bahèzre de Lanlay
Goureau
Jean Humblot
Albert Grivault
Loppin
Baudot

Q. **Are the Hospices de Beaune wines among the best wines of Burgundy?**

A. They are good wines but not great wines such as a Musigny, a Richebourg, a Romanée Conti, a Chambertin or a Clos de Vougeot of a good vintage.

Q. **Which are the best vineyards of Pommard?**

A. Les Epenòts (26 acres)
Les Rugiens Bas (13 acres)
Le Clos Blanc (11 acres)
They are the three *Têtes de Cuvée* but there are many *Premières Cuvées* which enjoy a well-deserved reputation among connoisseurs, such as the Clos de la Commaraine (10 acres), Les Petits-Epenots (51 acres) and Les Croix Noires (11 acres).

Q. **Which are the best vineyards of Volnay?**

A. Les Caillerets (36 acres)
Les Champans (28 acres)
Les Fremiets (16 acres)
La Angles (8·5 acres)
They are the *Têtes de Cuvée* and there is a score of *Premières Cuvées* producing good wines.

Q. **Which are the best vineyards of Monthélie?**

A. There are no *Têtes de Cuvée* and only a couple of *Premières Cuvées*.

Q. **Which are the best vineyards of Auxey-Duresses?**
A. Five *Deuxièmes Cuvées*.

Q. **Which are the best vineyards of Meursault?**
A. Les Santenots (22 acres), the only red wine *Tête de Cuvée*; it is usually sold as Volnay, the adjoining *Commune*.
Les Perrières, the only *Tête de Cuvée* for the white wines.
Les Genevrières (42·5 acres)
Les Charmes (39 acres), the two better known white *Premières Cuvées*.
La Goutte d'Or (11·5 acres), a very popular white *Deuxième Cuvée*.

Q. **Which are the best vineyards of Puligny-Montrachet?**
A. Le Montrachet, part of (10 acres), the only white *Tête de Cuvée*.
Le Chevalier Montrachet (15·5 acres)
Le Bâtard-Montrachet, part of (24 acres)
Les Combettes (17 acres)
Blagny-Blanc (11 acres) – all four white *Premières Cuvées*.

Q. **Which are the best vineyards of Chassagne-Montrachet?**
A. Le Montrachet, part of (10·5 acres), the only white *Tête de Cuvée*.
Le Bâtard-Montrachet, part of (32·5 acres), a white *Première Cuvée*.
Le Clos Saint-Jean (36 acres), the only red wine *Tête de Cuvée*.
La Maltroie (23 acres), a red wine *Première Cuvée*, where they now grow also white grapes and make a popular white wine marketed under the name of Château de la Maltroie.

Q. **Which is the best vineyard of Santenay?**
A. Les Gravières (62 acres), the only *Tête de Cuvée*.

Saône-et-Loire

Q. **What about the vineyards of the Saône-et-Loire Department?**
A. In the Saône-et-Loire Department there are two groups of hills known as Côte Chalonnaise and Côte Mâconnaise. The first 'takes over' from the Côte de Beaune at Chagny, beyond Santenay, and 'hands over' at Tournus to the Côte Mâconnaise, which carries on until Romanèche-Thorins and the Beaujolais. The vineyards of both Côtes all face the river Saône eastwards, the best of them being

planted with Pinots and the great majority with the commoner Gamay grape, for the red wines, and the Aligoté for the whites.

Q. **Which are the best wines of the Côte Chalonnaise?**
A. The red wine of Mercurey and the white wines of Rully and Montagny.

Q. **Which are the best wines of the Côte Mâconnaise?**
A. The red wine of Moulin-à-Vent and the white wines of Pouilly, Fuissé, Solutré, Loché and Vinzelles, usually sold as Pouilly-Fuissé.

Q. **Is Pouilly a town or a Commune?**
A. It is a mere hamlet in the *Commune* of Solutré.

Beaujolais

Q. **What about Beaujolais?**
A. The vineyards of the Beaujolais are more considerable than those of the Côtes Chalonnaise and Mâconnaise put together; they face the river Saône and extend to the south almost as far as Lyons.

Q. **Which are the best wines of the Beaujolais?**
A. They are, from north to south, those of Juliénas, Chenas, Fleurie, Chiroubles, Morgon and Brouilly. They are very nice wines indeed, but not aristocrats, and their chief asset is that they are most acceptable when quite young, which also means that they are less costly than wines which have to be nursed for a number of years. Unfortunately it also means that the demand for Beaujolais far exceeds its supply.

Q. **Are all Beaujolais wines red?**
A. They used to be, but there are white and *rosés* Beaujolais now.

Q. **Are the white wines of Beaujolais as good as the other white wines of Burgundy?**
A. They are made from the Aligoté grape, not Pinot Chardonnay, so they have neither the *bouquet* nor the breed of all the better white Burgundies; but they are pleasant *ordinaires* white wines.

Q. **Which are the best known of all white Burgundies?**

A. The wines of Chablis cannot compare in quality with the great white wines of the Côte d'Or, but they are better known than all others all over the world.

Chablis

Q. **Where is Chablis?**

A. Chablis is a nice little town on the banks of the river Serein in the Yonne Department; it is surrounded by chalk hills clothed in vineyards which produce a charming, light, elegant white wine which is most acceptable when quite young and yet one that may stand the test of time and gain by being kept ten years or even longer.

Q. **Do all Chablis wines come from Chablis?**

A. Unfortunately the supply of genuine Chablis is very much smaller than the demand and the name has such an appeal that it is used to sell a number of white wines which have no right to the name.

Q. **How much genuine Chablis is there?**

A. The vineyards of Chablis add up to less than 1,000 acres, less than 10% of the total Yonne vineyards, and their acreage is less every year. When the vines are spared by May frosts, which can be disastrous, and when all conditions are favourable, the vineyards of Chablis can produce the equivalent of half a million bottles of all grades of quality.

Q. **Which are the different qualities of Chablis?**

A. There are four officially recognised qualities of Chablis:
   (1) Chablis Grands Crus
   (2) Chablis Premiers Crus
   (3) Chablis
   (4) Petit Chablis or Bourgogne des environs de Chablis.

Q. **Which are the Chablis Grands Crus?**

A. Blanchot, Les Clos, Grenouilles, Valmur and Vaudésir.

Q. **Which are the Chablis Premiers Crus?**

A. Bougros, Chapelot, Fourchaume, Mont-de-Milieu, Montée de Tonnerre, Preuze, Vaulorent.

Q. **Are there any Châteaux in Burgundy as in the Médoc?**
A. There are a few Châteaux in Burgundy, such as Château-Gris, the Nuits Saint-Georges home of the de Lupés; but there are no Châteaux with important vineyards attached to them as in the Médoc.

Q. **Is there no Château-bottled Burgundy?**
A. There is Burgundy bottled by the proprietor of the vineyard but his home and/or cellars may be a long way from some of the vineyards he may own in different parts of the country. The wine is not described as Château-bottled but bottled at the 'Domaine', meaning on the estate where the vineyard's proprietor has his cellars.

Q. **Is there not a Château du Clos Vougeot?**
A. Indeed there is, and a fine Château it is now that it has been restored by the Confrérie des Chevaliers du Tastevin and is used by them as their headquarters. But it has nothing to do with the Clos de Vougeot's vines and wines.

Q. **Is there any sparkling Burgundy?**
A. There is a good deal of red sparkling Burgundy made in Burgundy, chiefly at Nuits St. Georges, and there is also some white sparkling Burgundy.

Q. **Which have been the best vintages of Burgundy of the twentieth century?**
A. The best Burgundy vintages have been the years 1900, 1904, 1906, 1911, 1915, 1926, 1928, 1929, 1934, 1937, 1945, 1947, 1949, 1952, 1953, 1955 and 1959.

Champagne

Q. **What is Champagne?**
A. Champagne is the sparkling wine made from grapes grown within a strictly defined part of the former Province of Champagne, now

known as *La Champagne délimitée*.

Q. **Whereabouts is it?**

A. About half way from Paris to Nancy, from west to east, and about half way from Amiens to Dijon, from north to south.

Q. **What makes Champagne sparkle?**

A. Champagne is made to sparkle by a second fermentation which takes place after the wine has been bottled and securely corked. The carbonic acid gas which is then produced cannot escape into the air, as it does when the fermentation takes place in a cask; it remains in solution in the wine until such time as the cork is removed and the wine poured out in glasses. Then the carbonic acid gas has its chance and gets away as fast as it can: as it rises to the surface of the wine in the glass, it carries tiny droplets of wine which are the bubbles.

Q. **Can this not be done anywhere else except in Champagne?**

A. It can be done and it is done in most wine-growing countries: there are a great many sparkling wines made in Europe; America, Australia and Africa, but there is only one genuine Champagne – the sparkling wine of Champagne vineyards.

Q. **But are there not other sparkling wines called Champagne?**

A. There are, but they cannot be offered for sale under the name of Champagne in France, England or Germany, for instance, as the name *Champagne* is protected by law in all three countries. In other lands, however, the manufacturers of sparkling wines have appropriated the name of Champagne for the sake of the prestige which attaches to the name, and they sell their sparkling wines as Australian Champagne, California Champagne, etc.

Q. **To what does Champagne owe the prestige that attaches to its name?**

A. Champagne owes its prestige and world-wide popularity first of all to the fact that it has been known ever since the seventeenth century – that is, very much longer than any of the other sparkling wines. Another and more important cause of the popularity of Champagne is the fact that Champagne is made not only with great care and skill, but from a wine that is more suitable than any other. The carbonic acid gas in all sparkling wines is exactly the same but it is the wine that matters most: it will still be there when most or all the carbonic acid gas has gone out of it. As it happens, the wine of the Champagne vineyards is quite different from those of Saumur or Burgundy, or Australia or California; better or not is a matter of opinion, but different and also more suitable for sparkling wines is a matter of fact.

Q. **Is all Champagne so much better than all other sparkling wines?**
A. Certainly not. There are good and bad wines made in Champagne as in all other vinelands and the Champagne that is better than other sparkling wines must be good Champagne.

Q. **Which is the best Champagne?**
A. The best Champagne is the best blend of wines made from the first pressings of none but the best Champagne grapes.

Q. **Which are the best Champagne grapes?**
A. They are noble Pinots, black or white, from the best vineyards of the Marne Department. There are in the Marne Department, as there are in the Gironde Department and elsewhere, small or great differences in the sub-soil, soil, aspect and elevation of all vineyards, and those differences are responsible for differences in the quality of the wines made from the same species of grapes. In the Marne Department the best vineyards are those of Verzenay, Sillery, Mailly, Ay-Champagne, Ambonnay, Bouzy and other first class vineyards of the Montagne de Reims and Valley of the Marne, where black Pinots are the rule; also Avize, Cramant and other *Communes* of the Côte des Blancs, where they grow white grapes only.

Q. **Why do they not sell Champagne under the name of vineyards or of Communes?**
A. Because Champagne is not, like the best Clarets, Burgundies, Hocks and Moselles, made from the grapes of any one *Commune* or vineyard. It is made from both black and white Pinot grapes from a number of different Champagne vineyards, 'married', assembled or blended into different *Cuvées*. It was the technique introduced by the famous Dom Pérignon, the Cellarer of the Benedictine

Abbey of Hautvilliers that overlooks the river Marne, facing
Epernay, and it has been practised in Champagne with conspicuous
success during the past two hundred and sixty years.

Q. **Is Champagne sold under the name of the man or firm responsible
for the blending of the wine and the making of the Cuvée?**

A. Not necessarily. All the well-known brands of Champagne are sold
under the name and brand of the firm which grew or bought the
grapes from which the wine was made, and blended the wine of
different vineyards as they thought best to make up *Cuvées,* which
differ in quality and price. There are also many *Cuvées* of Champagne bought ready-made by wine-merchants who sell them under
some brand which they have invented and registered so that no
competitor can offer Champagne under the same brand. Those
fancy brands are known in the wine trade as B.O.B., that is 'Buyer's
own Brands'.

Q. **How is it that they make a white wine in Champagne from black
grapes?**

A. Because the juice of those grapes is white, and when the grapes are
crushed or pressed at the time of the vintage their white juice is
run off the press right away without being given a chance to be
coloured by contact with the red pigment in the grapes' skins.

Q. **What is Champagne Rosé?**

A. It is a white Champagne which has been tinted pink by the addition
of a little red Champagne wine made from black grapes, mostly
from the vineyards of Bouzy and Trépail.

Q. **What kind of Champagne is called Blanc de Blancs?**

A. It is a sparkling Champagne made exclusively from white Pinot
Chardonnay grapes from the Champagne district known as Côte
des Blancs, around Avize: its vineyards are all white-grape vineyards.

Q. **Is a Blanc de Blancs Champagne a better wine?**

A. Better or not is a matter of individual appreciation: it has less body
and less lasting power than a sparkling Champagne which has been
made in the usual manner with the white juice of both black and

white Pinots; on the other hand it is lighter, sometimes even thin and sharp, usually, however, more elegant, and there are people who put on the credit side of Blanc de Blancs Champagne the fact that they can drink more of it with impunity than any other wine.

Q. **Is there a Blanc de Noirs Champagne?**
A. There is a very little Champagne made exclusively from black grapes: it has more body but less *finesse* than the Blanc de Blancs, and there is no likelihood of its ever becoming popular.

Q. **Which were the best vintages of the twentieth century?**
A. They were: 1900, 1904, 1906, 1911, 1915, 1920, 1921, 1926, 1928, 1929, 1934, 1937, 1942, 1945, 1947, 1949, 1952, 1953, 1955 and 1959.

Q. **What is Vintage Champagne?**
A. Vintage Champagne is a blend of Champagne wines from different Champagne vineyards all made in the same year or 'vintage', a year when the sun had been kind and the grapes were beautifully ripe at vintage time. This does not happen, unfortunately, every year.

Q. **What happens when the sun is not kind?**
A. Grapes are gathered from which a wine is made which needs a little help to be really nice: it gets this help in the form of some of the best Champagne of former years, kept in reserve for the purpose; this is how non-vintage Champagne is made, a blend of wines of different years as well as of different vineyards.

Q. **Is a non-vintage Champagne an inferior wine?**
A. Certainly not. It has not got the distinctive or characteristic quality which a vintage Champagne owes to the climate conditions of the year or vintage when it was made, but the great Champagne Houses with considerable reserves of fine wines can and do sell *Cuvées* of non-vintage Champagne of real merit, always less expensive and often better value than many vintage *Cuvées*.

Q. **Is a Magnum of Champagne better than a bottle?**
A. A Magnum is two bottles and two are better than one. As regards the quality of the wine in Magnums and bottles, it is exactly the same at the time of the bottling and for some time. After a few years, how-

ever, the wine in the Magnum will be fresher, hence better, than the same wine in the bottle, and much better than the same wine in half bottles.

Q. **What is an Imperial pint of Champagne?**

A. An Imperial pint of Champagne holds three-quarters of a bottle, 60 centilitres, to the bottle's 80 and the half bottle's 40. The Imperial pint was in great demand in Victorian times, when the more abstemious wine connoisseurs considered a bottle a little too much for one person, but a half bottle not nearly enough.

Q. **Are there any Champagne bottles larger than the Magnum?**

A. Indeed, there are, and they bear quite colourful names, but nobody knows who chose those names and why:
Jeroboam contains 4 Champagne bottles or 0·70 gallon
Rehoboam contains 6 Champagne bottles or 1·05 gallons
Methuselah contains 8 Champagne bottles or 1·40 gallons
Salmanazar contains 12 Champagne bottles or 2·10 gallons
Balthazar contains 16 Champagne bottles or 2·80 gallons
Nebuchadnezzar contains 20 Champagne bottles or 3·50 gallons

Q. **Is the Champagne any better in such large bottles?**

A. No, it is not. The Jeroboams of some Champagne shippers are bottle fermented, like the bottles and Magnums, but the Champagne in all the larger bottles is decanted from bottles or Magnums. Those outsize bottles are used for show purposes only.

Q. **What about quarter bottles of Champagne?**

A. Champagne in a quarter bottle – sometimes called a 'baby' or a 'nip' – has to be decanted, which does not harm the wine but does not add life to it. The quarter bottle holds one glass of Champagne only and it is mostly called for by somewhat mean invalids who will not share a half bottle with their nurse or doctor.

Q. **What is the meaning of Nature and Brut on some Champagne Labels?**

A. They mean that the wine in the bottle has not been 'liqueured' or sweetened at all, or very little.

Q. **What is the meaning of Extra Sec, Sec, and Demi-Sec?**

A. Extra Sec means a dry Champagne, a wine with very little 'liqueur-ing' or added sweetness. Sec means 'dry' when talking of the weather, but it means 'sweet' when talking of Champagne; Demi-Sec does not mean half dry but very sweet.

Q. **Is there not a non-sparkling white wine called Champagne Nature?**
A. There used to be such a wine, but according to recent French legislation it must be marketed now as *Vin blanc de la Champagne.* When not otherwise qualified, the name 'Champagne' must not be used for any wine other than sparkling Champagne.

Q. **Is there much still wine made in Champagne?**
A. There is a great deal of still wine made in Champagne, both red and white, both fine and homely. Still wines made from commoner grapes are *ordinaires*, often *très ordinaires*: they are inexpensive and drunk in the homes of the people who make them and the local *bistros*. There are also some fine quality red table wines made entirely from the black grapes of Bouzy, Ambonnay and Trépail in much the same way as Claret is made; there are also some fine quality white table wines made entirely from white grapes from Avize, Cramant, Le Mesnil and Oger, in much the same way as Chablis is made, but those still Champagne wines being made from the same very high-price grapes from which sparkling Champagne is made, are too costly to be a commercial proposition: they are made in small quantities only, chiefly for the Champagne shippers themselves, and a few of their friends.

Alsace

Q. **Are the wines of Alsace newcomers in England?**
A. Yes, they had not been heard of in England, or for that matter, anywhere else between 1871, when the Germans took Alsace from France, and 1919 when Alsace became French again.

Q. **Was no wine made in Alsace during all those years?**
A. A great deal of wine was made in Alsace, but all that was not drunk by the Alsatians themselves had to go to Germany; there it was drunk by the Germans or sold by them as Hock, not Alsace.

Q. **Is Alsace wine like Hock?**

A. It looks like Hock, which means nothing since Hock looks like most other white wines; and Alsace wine is sold in long tapering green bottles which look like Moselle bottles; but, again, this does not mean anything, since it is the wine in the bottle that matters and there is a whole range of Alsace wines with a personality entirely their own.

Q. **Where are the vineyards of Alsace?**

A. They are scattered along the foothills of the Vosges Mountains, facing a wide plain and the Rhine beyond, from the Thur Valley, south of Colmar and north of Mulhouse, as far as Strasbourg and a little beyond, on the way to the German Palatinate vineyards.

Q. **Which are the best vineyards of Alsace?**

A. They are those of a number of *Communes* or villages, most of them in the Haut-Rhin Department (Colmar) and a very few in the Bas-Rhin Department (Strasbourg), chiefly Ribeauvillé, Riquewihr, Mittelwihr, Hunawihr, Ammerschwihr, Sigolsheim and Guebwiller, but their wines are not sold under the name of the native village or vineyard: they are sold under the name of the grape from which the wine in the bottle was made, without any indication of where those grapes were actually grown.

Q. **Which are the grapes from which the best wines of Alsace are made?**

A. They are the Riesling for quality wines with greater breed and better balanced than most; the Traminer and Gewurztraminer, for quality wines that are somewhat richer and more fragrant; the Muscat, for quality wines with less breed but more *bouquet*; the Pinot and Pinot Gris, also called Tokay d'Alsace, for quality wines with less *finesse* but more flavour; the Sylvaner for quality wines with less body but greater freshness and liveliness. There are a number of other species of grapes grown in Alsace, such as the Knipperlé, Chasselas, Burger, etc., from which the more ordinary and cheaper wines are made.

Q. **Is Zwicker one of the grapes of Alsace?**

A. No. Zwicker is the name of white Alsace wines made of a blend of

71

different grapes; and when they use rather more of the better grapes in the blend, they call it Edelzwicker.

Q. **What is Kitterle?**

A. It is the local name, used mostly in the Guebwiller Valley, of a Zwicker or blend in which there is a great deal more Chasselas wine than wines of other grapes.

Q. **Are none of the wines of Alsace sold under the name of their native vineyard?**

A. There are a few wines sold under the name of their native vineyard. Thus Hugel, of Riquewhir, sell a blend of Riesling, Pinot Gris and Muscat grapes grown in a vineyard on a slope immediately south of Riquewhir, under the label 'Sporen', which is the name of the vineyard. Kanzlerberg, Kaepfferkopf and Schoenenburg are also names of vineyards which are to be seen on the labels of Alsace wines.

Q. **Is the name of the shipper of the wine of great importance?**

A. The name of the shipper, which is always given on the wine label together with the name of the village or town where the said shipper has his offices and cellars, but not necessarily his vineyards, is of great importance. There are shippers who sell none but the wines of their own vineyards, whilst others own no vineyards and ship the wines they pick and choose where and when they think best.

Q. **Which have been the best vintages for Alsace wines since 1929?**

A. 1934, 1937, 1938, 1942, 1943, 1947, 1952, 1953, 1954, 1955, 1957, 1959.

Q. **Are there any wines made north of Alsace, in Lorraine?**

A. Yes, there are quite a number of wines made in the valleys of the rivers Moselle, Meurthe and Meuse in Lorraine, near Epinal, Toul and Bar-le-Duc – red wines, white wines called *vin gris* locally – but none of them has any claim to the wine connoisseur's attention.

Q. **Why is this?**

A. Because the climate is not suitable for growing quality grapes and quality wines. Lorraine wines are mostly of low alcohlic strength and they have little or no *bouquet*; they can be however, most acceptable and really refreshing on a hot summer's day.

La Loire

Q. **Are there many vineyards in the valley of the Loire?**
A. There are roughly 500,000 acres of vineyards 'along the 629 miles of the Loire from the Cévennes to the Atlantic, many of them producing *ordinaires* wines only, whilst others produce both *ordinaires* and quality wines.

Q. **Which are the vineyards of the Loire which produce quality wines?**
A. They are the vineyards of the Upper Loire, Pouilly-sur-Loire, Sancerre, Quincy, Reuilly and St. Pourçain-sur-Sioule in the Cher and Nièvre Departments; the vineyards of Touraine in the Indre-et-Loire Department; the vineyards of Anjou in the Maine-et-Loire Department; and the vineyards of the Lower Loire in the Loire-Atlantique, Maine-et-Loire and Deux Sèvres Departments.

Q. **Do these four sections of the Loire Valley produce much quality wine?**
A. They do. Here is the average production of white, red and *rosés* quality wines of all four sections:

	White Wines (Gallons)	Red or Rosés Wines (Gallons)	Total (Gallons)
Upper Loire	550,000	—	550,000
Touraine	2,000,000	2,000,000	4,000,000
Anjou	4,500,000	3,500,000	8,000,000
Lower Loire	3,450,000	—	3,450,000
	10,500,000	5,500,000	16,000,000

Upper Loire

Q. **Which are the best wines of the Upper Loire?**
A. They are the Blanc Fumé or Pouilly Blanc Fumé of Pouilly-sur-Loire.

Q. **Is Pouilly Fumé more or less the same as Pouilly Fuissé?**
A. It is not. Pouilly Fumé is a white wine made exclusively from Sauvig-

non grapes from the vineyards of Pouilly-sur-Loire in the Nièvre Department, but Pouilly Fuissé is made from Pinot Chardonnay grapes grown in the vineyards of Pouilly, Fuissé and Solutré in the Department of Saône-et-Loire.

Q. **Where is Pouilly-sur-Loire?**

A. Pouilly-sur-Loire is a little town upon the right bank of the Loire, north of Nevers and south of Orléans. Its vineyards were completely destroyed by the phylloxera during the 'Nineties, and they have never regained their former importance. Coming to the last houses of Pouilly itself, and cultivated in two of the nearby villages, the vineyards of Pouilly-sur-Loire add up to just about 1,000 acres; but there are only some 325 acres with Sauvignon grapes producing on an average 46,000 gallons of white quality wines a year, and 675 acres with Chasselas and other grapes producing on an average 154,000 gallons of more *ordinaires* wines, a total of 200,000 gallons. There are about 400 *vignerons* in Pouilly, and the nearby villages, who are entitled to sell their Sauvignon-made wines as Pouilly-Fumé or Blanc-Fumé de Pouilly-sur-Loire; none of them, bar one, has any sizeable quantity of the wine to sell.

Q. **Who is the one vigneron with a large holding?**

A. He is the Baron de Ladoucette, his home, the Château du Nozet, and his holding 35 acres (25 acres Sauvignon, 10 acres Chasselas).

Q. **What happens to the wine which is made from Chasselas or other grapes?**

A. It is sold as Pouilly-sur-Loire white wine, without any mention of Fumé.

Q. **Has Fumé anything to do with smoky flavour or look?**

A. Not at all. Blanc-Fumé happens to be the name given locally to the grapes otherwise called Sauvignon.

Q. **Where is Sancerre?**

A. Sancerre is a little town, complete with its own Château, sitting atop the highest (500 feet above the Loire) of a range of hills of the Cher Department on the left of the Loire, known as the hills of the Sancerrois or Sancerre country.

Q. **Are there as many vineyards in the Sancerre country as in and around Pouilly-sur-Loire on the other side of the river?**

A. There are a great many more vineyards in the Sancerrois. Besides the vineyards of Sancerre's own rock pedestal or hill, there are thirteen other *Communes* with vineyards upon the other Sancerrois hills which add up to 1,500 acres, two-thirds of which (1,000 acres) produce quality wines entitled to the *Appellation contrôlée* Sancerre.

Q. **Are there any Communes or villages of the Sancerrois which produce better wines than the rest?**

A. Yes, the wines of Chavignol and Amigny, two hamlets of the *Commune* of Sancerre, also Bue and Verdigny, two of the nearby *Communes*, are reputed to produce white wines of greater *finesse* or distinction than most other white wines of the Sancerrois.

Q. **Where is Quincy?**

A. Quincy is some 12½ miles west of Bourges on the left bank of the river Cher. Its vineyards add up to 525 acres, of which 375 acres are under Sauvignon grapes. They can produce 100,000 gallons of wine in a year, a sunny year free from late spring frosts.

Q. **Where is Reuilly?**

A. Reuilly is a village some 6 miles west of Quincy with merely 62 acres of Sauvignon-planted vineyards which produce on an average 1,300 gallons of quality white wine per annum.

Q. **Are all the white quality wines of the Upper Loire alike?**

A. They all have a certain family likeness due to the fact that they are all made from the same grape, the Sauvignon, but they do differ from one another in *bouquet* and flavour according to the nature of the soil of the different vineyards which produce them.

Touraine

Q. **Where is Touraine?**

A. Touraine is a gracious land of rivers and vales, Châteaux and gardens, vineyards and orchards: it has often been called *Le Jardin de la France*. The whole of the Indre-et-Loire Department and parts of

75

the Loire-et-Cher Department cover today the ground that used to be the Province of Touraine. The Loire flows through the whole of its length, from Blois to Candes, where the Vienne river joins the Loire and Touraine joins Anjou. The capital city of Touraine is Tours: its first bishop, St. Martin, who died at Candes in A.D. 397, is the Patron Saint of London's Worshipful Company of Vintners.

Q. **Which are the best wines of Touraine?**
A. The best white wines of Touraine are those of Vouvray, on the right bank of the Loire, and of Montlouis, on the left bank. The best red wines of Touraine are the wines of Bourgueil, on the right bank of the Loire, and of Chinon, on the left.

Q. **Where is Vouvray?**
A. Vouvray is a sprawling riverside town at the foot of a great lime bluff which is honeycombed with cellars and the dwellings of some of Vouvray's population. The vineyards of Vouvray are planted on the top of that cliff as well as by the Loire and the small Cissé river which joins the Loire a little below Vouvray. The Vouvray vineyards are those of the *Commune* of Vouvray itself, and also the vineyards of the *Communes* of Rochecorbon, Sainte Radegonde, and half-a-dozen more in the immediate vicinity.

Q. **How important are the vineyards of Vouvray?**
A. The vineyards of Vouvray and of the adjoining *Communes* entitled to sell their wine as Vouvray add up to 3,750 acres which are owned by about one thousand different *vignerons*; it means that all of them have small holdings only.

Q. **How much Vouvray wine is there every year?**
A. The yield of the Vouvray vineyards varies greatly from year to year but on an average they produce 726,000 gallons of white wines made from Pineau de la Loire grapes and entitled to the Vouvray *Appellation Contrôlée*, some of them still and others sparkling, some of them quite dry table wines and others sweet dessert wines.

Q. **Are there any Châteaux or Estates famed for the quality of their wines?**
A. There are no Châteaux but there are a number of Estates known as

'Clos' with a well-deserved reputation for the quality and reliability of their wines, such as Clos Le Mont, Clos Moncontour, Clos du Bourg, Clos Le Paradis, etc., in the *Commune* of Vouvray; Clos de la Taisserie, Clos Château Chevrier, etc., in the *Commune* of Rochecorbon; Clos de Chaillemont, Clos du Fougeray, etc., in the *Commune* of Vernon.

Q. **Which have been the best vintages of the twentieth century at Vouvray?**
A. 1900, 1904, 1906, 1908, 1911, 1914, 1919, 1921, 1924, 1928, 1929, 1933, 1934, 1937, 1942, 1943, 1945, 1947, 1949, 1952, 1953, 1955, 1959.

Q. **Where is Montlouis?**
A. Montlouis is on the other side of the Loire, opposite Vouvray, where the river Cher flows into the Loire. Its vineyards cover 1,250 acres. Their soil and their grapes are exactly the same as those of Vouvray and, previous to 1938, the wines of Montlouis were sold under the better-known name of Vouvray. Now, however, they must be sold under their own *Appellation Contrôlée* of Montlouis.

Q. **What is the average production of the Montlouis vineyards?**
A. Their average production is 33,000 gallons a year, a little less than half the quantity of white wines on the other side of the Loire with the Vouvray *Appellation contrôlée*.

Q. **What is a Fillette?**
A. A *Fillette* is the name given in Touraine to a half bottle.

Q. **Which are the best red wines of Touraine?**
A. They are the wines of St. Nicholas de Bourgueil and of Chinon.

Q. **Where is St. Nicholas de Bourgueil?**
A. It is a village, the vineyards of which produce the best red wines of all from what may be called the Bourgueil country, a stretch of rising table-land from the right bank of the Loire some 15 miles long from Saint Patrice to St. Nicholas de Bourgueil: there are some 3,000 acres planted in Cabernet franc or Breton grapes producing on an average 660,000 gallons of red wine entitled to the *Appellation contrôlée* Bourgueil, but there is only one-third (220,000 gallons)

which is marketed under and entitled to the name of St. Nicholas de Bourgueil.

Q. **What sort of wine is the red wine of Bourgueil?**

A. It is a wine deep ruby in colour, of low alcoholic strength (from 9·5° to 10·5°) and possessing a most attractive *bouquet* as well as a pleasant flavour of its own: it cannot be called one of the great wines of France, but one of the nicest.

Q. **Where is Chinon?**

A. Chinon is on the Vienne, just before that river flows into the Loire, at Candes.

Q. **Are the vineyards of Chinon very important?**

A. They are, that is if we call Chinon vineyards all those of the valley of the Vienne above and below Chinon itself. But there are not more than 1,250 acres of Cabernet franc vineyards, with an average production of 220,000 gallons of red wine entitled to the *Appellation contrôlée* Chinon provided their alcoholic strength is not below 9·5°.

Q. **Which are the best wines of Chinon?**

A. They are the wines made from vineyards on the right bank of the river Vienne, downstream from Chinon as far as the left bank of the Loire, a stretch of country known to Rabelais and to this day as *Le pays Véron,* with Beaumont-en-Véron as its central and best wine *Commune.* La Roche Honneur, Château de Danzay and Les Pouilles are three of its best vineyards.

Q. **What sort of wine is the red wine of Chinon?**

A. It is very much like its cousin from the other side of the Loire, the red wine of Bourgueil, but its *bouquet* is more reminiscent of violets, Bourgueil's of wallflowers.

Anjou

Q. **Where is Anjou?**

A. Anjou, the cradle of the Plantagenet kings of England, lies between Touraine and Brittany, smaller than Brittany, much larger than

Touraine, and producing a great deal more quality wine than either.

Q. **Does Anjou produce more white wines than red?**
A. Yes, Anjou produces about five times as much white as red and about
. twice as much *rosé* wine as red. There are some 40,000 acres of vineyards in Anjou which produce wines with an *Appellation contrôlée*:
25,000 acres of Chenin blanc grapes for quality white wines; 5,000
acres of Breton or Cabernet de la Loire grapes producing quality
red wines; and 10,000 acres with a variety of grapes for quality
rosés wines.

Q. **Which are the best white wines of Anjou?**
A. They are the wines of Saumur, on the left bank of the Loire, near
the Touraine border; and the wines of the Coteaux du Layon and
Coteaux de L'Aubance, two of the Loire tributaries south of the
Loire; also the vineyards of the Coteaux de la Loire, north of the
river.

Q. **Are the wines of Saumur still or sparkling?**
A. There is much sparkling Saumur and it is better known in England
than the still wines of Saumur, but the quantity of still Saumur
wines – white, red and *rosés* – is much greater than that of the sparkling wine. All the better still white wines are made from Chenin
blanc grapes, the original Plant d'Anjou, and the same as the grape
which is called in nearby Touraine Pinot de la Loire. The alcoholic
strength of their wines must not be below 9·5° if they are to be given
the *Appellation contrôlée* Saumur, whereas the *vins rosés* need not be
over 9°; the red wines must not be below 10°.

Q. **Are the white wines of the Coteaux du Layon better than those of
Saumur?**
A. Yes, most of the white wines of the Valley of the Layon are better
wines, although made from the same grape – the Chenin blanc – but
with greater care from grapes picked as late as possible, so that they
may be fully ripe or even over-ripe; this means that the better white
wines of the Coteaux du Layon are both sweeter and finer wines.

Q. **Which are the best wines of the Coteaux du Layon?**
A. They are the wines of the vineyards of Rochefort-sur-Loire known

as *Quarts de Chaume* and *La Guillaumerie;* also the wines of the best vineyards of Thouarcé-Bonnezeaux (*La Petite Croix* and *Châteaux de Fesle*); Faye (*Château de Montbenault*); Rablay (*Château de la Roche*); Beaulieu and Saint-Aubin-de-Luigné (*La Saulaie, La Haie Longue* and *Château Fresnaye*).

Q. **Which are the best wines of the Coteaux de l'Aubance?**

A. They are the white wines of Juigné-sur-Loire and Murs, but there are fewer vineyards and much less wine made in the Valley of the Aubance than in the Valley of the Layon. The Aubance wines are similar to those of the Layon Coteaux but not nearly so well known outside Angers, Tours and Paris.

Q. **What about the *rosés* wines of Anjou?**

A. The *rosés* wines of Anjou have become extremely popular in France and overseas since the end of World War II. There are more than 3 million gallons sold every year of two sorts; one better and dearer than the other is made from Cabernet de la Loire grapes, and the other, a distinctly commoner and not always so distinctly cheaper wine, which is made from Groslot, Gamay or other commoner species of grapes. The first are always sold as *Cabernet rosé d'Anjou* or *Cabernet rosé de Saumur*, whereas the other is sold as *Rosé d'Anjou* without any mention of its parentage.

Q. **Which are the best wines of the Coteaux de la Loire?**

A. There are Coteaux or hills on both the north and south sides of the Loire but, in Anjou, when one speaks of the Coteaux de la Loire one means the hills of the right or north side of the Loire, south-west of Angers. Most of the vineyards of the Coteaux de la Loire produce white, red and *rosés* wines which lack *finesse* or distinction, with one very notable exception in favour of the vineyards of Savennières, a charming little village by the Loire some 9½ miles from Angers. There are two vineyards of Savennières which enjoy a well-deserved reputation. They are La Coulée de Serrant, a walled vineyard of nearly 10 acres, and La Roche aux Moines, a vineyard shared by ten different owners, whilst La Coulée de Serrant belongs to one proprietor only, which is always much more satisfactory from the point of view of the consumer.

The Lower Loire

Q. **Which are the vineyards of the Lower Loire?**

A. They are the vineyards both north and south of the river Loire on its last lap before Nantes on its way to the Atlantic. North of the Loire the best vineyards are those above and below the town of Ancenis, in the Loire–Atlantique Department, close to the border of Anjou; south of the Loire, to the east and south-east of Nantes, they are the wines of the Sèvre-et-Maine country, mostly in the Maine-et-Loire Department, above and below Liré. They cover 20,000 acres, about half of them north and half south of the Loire, which produce on an average 3,450,000 gallons of white wines every year.

Q. **Which are the best white wines of the Lower Loire?**

A. They are the white wines which are entitled to one or the other of three *Appellations contrôlées: Muscadet-des-Coteaux-de-la-Loire* (150,000 gallons), *Muscadet-de-Sèvre-et-Maine* (1,750,000 gallons) and *Muscadet* (750,000 gallons). All must be made exclusively from Muscadet grapes.

Q. **Is the Muscadet grape one of the aristocrats among grapes?**

A. No, it is one of the commoner sorts which came to the Loire from Burgundy, where it is called Melon; it was renamed Muscadet in Brittany and it produces a light and pleasant white wine, with little or no *bouquet* – a wine which was very little known in France, outside Brittany, before 1914 and had never been heard of outside France before 1939. It has since become quite popular in England.

Q. **Are the best Muscadets sold under the name of their native village or Chàteau?**

A. Not in England: the best are those which have been selected with greater care and professional knowledge by the wine merchants who sell them under their own name or registered brands.

Arbois

Q. **Where is Arbois?**

A. Arbois is a charming little old-world town, the birthplace of Louis Pasteur who deserves much more from humanity than having his name associated with pasteurised milk. Arbois nestles in a bower of vineyards, most of them facing south-west and all of them sheltered by the fir-clad Jura mountains standing between France and Switzerland, in the Jura Department.

Q. **Are there many vineyards in the Jura Department?**

A. There are about 6,800 acres of vineyards in the Jura Department, most of them dotted along an irregular imaginary line running from north-east to south-west, that is from Salins to Arbois and then to Pupillin, Poligny, Ménétru, Château Chalon and L'Etoile, above Lons-le-Saulnier.

Q. **What sorts of wine do they make in the Jura?**

A. They make a number of different wines: most of them are red, white and *rosés* table wines which vary from homely to fair and even fine in quality. The red wines are mostly made from Poulsard grapes, all the better white wines from white Savagnin grapes and the *rosés* wines from white Savagnin grapes pressed at the same time as red Poulsard or Gamay grapes. They also make at Arbois some sparkling wine which enjoys a fair measure of local reputation. The Jura wines, however, which are more typical and as such more deserving of the wine connoisseur's attention are the Vin Jaune and the Vin de Paille.

Q. **What is Vin Jaune?**

A. The Vin Jaune of the Jura is a dry white wine, not 'paper white' of course, but golden. It is made not from over-ripe grapes but from fully mature and perfectly sound grapes, such as are available only when there has been a fine sunny summer. The grapes are pressed and their sweet juice is fermented in a somewhat peculiar manner, according to the local traditional technique. It is kept in cask longer than other white wines usually are and it acquires during its slower and longer fermentation a higher alcoholic strength and a more highly developed *bouquet* than any of the other wines of the Jura. Chilled as an *apéritif*, is the best way to serve Vin Jaune, in the opinion of many a connoisseur.

Q. **What is a Vin de Paille?**

A. The Jura Vin de Paille is a golden dessert wine which can only be made in the sunniest years from carefully selected over-ripe white Savagnin grapes. When they are picked the grapes are laid on straw mats – hence the 'paille' or straw – in the sun and, as they los some of their moisture during that stage but none of their sugar, their juice is very much sweeter when they are crushed in the wine-press and, of course, there is much less of it than if the grapes had been pressed as soon as picked. The best Vin de Paille of the Jura is made at or near Château Chalon.

Q. **Is Château Chalon the name of a castle?**
A. No, it is the name of a village and of its vineyards, between Ménétru and Voiteur, south of Arbois.

Q. **How important is the production of quality wines in the Jura Department?**
A. About 30% of Jura wines are quality wines with an *Appellation d'origine*, and fully half of them are entitled to *Appellation contrôlée Arbois*.

Q. **Which are the other Appellations contrôlées of the Jura?**
A. They are Château Chalon, L'Etoile and Côtes du Jura and they, like the wines of Arbois, are entitled to the *Appellation contrôlée* only if the alcoholic strength of their various wines is not below 10° for the table wines, red, white or *rosés*; 11·5° for the Vins Jaunes; and 15° for the Vins de Paille.

Q. **What is Vin Fou?**
A. It is the registered name of a sparkling Arbois wine which is made and marketed by the oldest firm of growers and merchants of Arbois, Henri Maire.

Q. **What is Macoin?**
A. It is the registered name of a cordial made of a blend of concentrated grape juice of Jura grapes and the local Marc, a spirit distilled from the husks of the grapes after they have been pressed to make wine.

Rhône

Q. **Are there many vineyards in the Valley of the Rhône?**
A. Yes, there are a great many, practically all the way from the snow-

capped Valais heights, the Swiss birthplace of the great river, to sunny Provence, where the Phoenicians first planted vines, before Rome was built.

Q. **Which are the Rhône vineyards, in France, which produce the best wines?**

A. They are the vineyards upon the right and left banks of the Rhône from south of Lyons to north of Avignon, a distance of about 125 miles by road. They bring forth every year a great deal of wine of fair quality, table wines, red and white and *rosés*, which are entitled to the *Appellation d'origine* Côtes du Rhône. They also bring forth a much smaller proportion of fine quality wines entitled to an *Appellation contrôlée* of their own, the best-known of them being Côte Rôtie, Condrieu, Château Grillet, Hermitage, Croze-Hermitage, Châteauneuf-du-Pape and Tavel.

Q. **Where is Côte Rôtie?**

A. Côte Rôtie is the name given to a range of hills upon the right bank of the Rhône, above Ampuis, and only a little way south of Vienne, on the opposite side of the river. According to tradition, locally accepted as fact, the first vineyard was planted above Ampuis in 600 B.C. Today the terraced vineyards of the Côte Rôtie cling to the sharp slopes of the Côte Brune, where the black Syrah grapes are the only ones grown, and of the Côte Blonde, next to the other, where there are rather more white Viognier grapes grown than black Syrah. Côte Rôtie is in the Rhône Department.

Q. **Where is Condrieu?**

A. Condrieu is a little town on the right bank of the Rhône at the southern tip of the Rhône Department, some 20 miles below Lyons. It has been famous for a great many years for the excellence of the white wines of its vineyards: nine-tenths of their grapes are white Viognier grapes. The white Condrieu wine is one of the few white wines which gain body, *bouquet* and power with age.

Q. **Where is Château Grillet?**

A. Château Grillet is the name of a remarkable white wine which is made from the white Viognier grapes of a small vineyard (2½ acres only) high above Condrieu. The white wine of Château Grillet has long been praised as one of the great white wines of France and of the world, but there is so little of it that few people have had the chance to taste it, in England, where it was practically unobtainable before 1961.

Q. **What happened in 1961?**
A. The owner of Château Grillet appointed for the first time in history an agent in London and allotted to him a small quantity of Château Grillet for sale in the British Isles.

Q. **Where is Hermitage?**
A. Hermitage – or Ermitage, both spellings are accepted in France – is a hill which must be made of hard stuff since it still stands where it has stood for centuries in the way of the rushing waters of the Rhône and makes them change their course. It rises above the little town of Tain l'Ermitage, on the left bank of the river, opposite Tournon. The slopes of the Ermitage Hill are covered with vineyards owned by many *vignerons*, most of them with very small holdings to which they can and do give their unstinted and intelligent care. Two-thirds of the grapes grown on the Ermitage Hill are black Syrah grapes and one-third white Marsanne and Roussane grapes.

Q. **Which are the best vineyards of Hermitage?**
A. They are Les Bessards and Le Méal; next comes Greffieux, La Chapelle, Les Murets and a few more which are responsible for all the best red Ermitage wines. As regards the white wines, the best and the best-known is the wine of Chante-Alouette.

Q. **Where is Croze-l'Ermitage?**
A. It is in the *Commune* or parish nearest to Tain l'Ermitage. Its vineyards adjoin those of Tain l'Ermitage and produce red wines of a very similar character, although often a little lighter.

Q. **Where is Mercurol?**
A. Mercurol is the parish nearest to Tain l'Ermitage on the south side. Its vineyards produce red wines of the same character as those of the Ermitage Hill, but of somewhat less remarkable quality.

Q. **Where is Cornas?**

A. Cornas is in the Ardèche Department, immediately south of Tournon. Its vineyards produce red wines of fair quality not unlike some of the red wines of the Ermitage Hill on the opposite bank of the Rhône.

Q. **Where is St. Péray?**
A. St. Péray is also in the Ardèche Department, below Cornas. Its vineyards produce some very pleasant white wines, both still and sparkling.

Q. **Where is Châteauneuf-du-Pape?**
A. Châteauneuf-du-Pape is the name of a rather uninteresting little town of the Vaucluse Department, on the same side of the Rhône as Tain l'Ermitage but 85 miles further south. It is also the name given to the red wines made from grapes grown in the 100,000 acres of vineyards stretching from Orange to Avignon. They produce on an average 40 million gallons of wine every year, 90% red and 10% white, some 30% of them being quality wines entitled to the *Appellation contrôlée* Châteauneuf-du-Pape.

Q. **Which are the best wines of Châteauneuf-du-Pape?**
A. They are the red wines sold under the name of their native vineyard and bottled at the Château or Estate, such as Château de la Nerthe, Château Fines Roches, Château Fortia, the three to enjoy the greatest reputation in the British Isles; also Condorcet, Nallys, Vaudieu, La Cardine, Le Boucou and Les Cabrières.

Q. **What about Gigondas?**
A. Gigondas is the name of one of the parishes of the Vaucluse Department; its vineyards produce a very nice red wine which has been given an *Appellation contrôlée* of its own: Côtes du Rhône Gigondas.

Q. **Where is Tavel?**
A. Tavel is a small town on the right bank of the Rhône in the Gard Department. Its name has long been known to wine connoisseurs on account of the excellence of its *vin rosé*.

Q. **Why should Tavel *Rosé* be better than other *rosés* wines?**
A. Chiefly because of the soil and of its vineyards; it is made up of

sand, lime and flints, and how. any vines can grow in such poor soil is little short of a miracle – but they do and they bring forth a wine with greater *finesse* than most.

Q. **Are there any other quality wines made in the same part of the Gard Department?**

A. Yes, the vineyards of Lirac and Chusclan produce some very fair wines which have been given their own *Appellation contrôlée*.

Q. **Are there any quality wines made in the Rhône Valley besides the Côtes du Rhône wines?**

A. Yes, there are some interesting wines, wines of fair quality but not great wines, made along the course of the Rhône from its entry into France soon after leaving Geneva and before it reaches Lyons. Some of the vineyards of Savoie, on the left of the Rhône, and some of those on its right, in the Bugey, might qualify as Rhône wines. The only wine of note, however, from vineyards actually by the Rhône-side, is the wine of Seyssel.

Q. **Where is Seyssel?**

A. Seyssel is an old town about a third of the way from the Franco-Swiss frontier and Lyons. It sits atop a cleft rock with vineyards on both sides of the Rhône – those on the right being in the Ain Department and those on the left in the Haute Savoie. The best Seyssel wines are white wines, both still and sparkling, which are made from white Roussette grapes. To be entitled to their *Appellation contrôlée* the still white wine of Seyssel must not be below 10° in alcoholic strength, and the sparkling wine not below 8·5°.

Q. **Which have been the best Rhône vintages of the twentieth century?**

A. 1900, 1901, 1904, 1906, 1908, 1911, 1914, 1916, 1918, 1921, 1924, 1926, 1929, 1933, 1934, 1936, 1938, 1939, 1943, 1945, 1947, 1948, 1949, 1952, 1955, 1956, 1959, 1961.

Provence

Q. **Where is Provence?**

A. ·Provence is the easternmost part of the south of France, which includes that part of the Mediterranean seaboard, and its hinterland, colonised by the Romans more than two thousand years ago and named by them *Provincia Romana*. It stretches from the Savoy Alps to the sea, from north to south, and from the Italian frontier to the Lower Rhône Valley from east to west. Four French Departments are wholly or partly in Provence: the Var, Bouches-du-Rhône, Alpes Maritimes and Basses Alpes. The acreage of their vineyards and their potential production of wine are as follows:

	Var	Bouches-du-Rhône	Alpes Maritimes	Basses Alpes
Acres	162,500	25,000	8,000	7,000
Gallons	55,000,000	33,000,000	1,000,000	2,000,000
Quality Wines	1%	0·3%	0·8%	Nil

Q. **Which are the quality wines of the Var?**

A. They are the white wines with the *Appellation contrôléee* Côtes de Provence; also the white, red and *rosés* wines of Bandol and La Côte des Maures.

Q. **Which are the quality wines of the Bouches-du-Rhône?**

A. They are the red, white and *rosés* wines of Cassis, between Marseilles and Toulon; also the white wines of Château Simone, at Palette, near Aix-en-Provence.

Q. **Which are the quality wines of the Alpes Maritimes?**

A. They are the wines of Bellet, near Nice, which used to be better known, and perhaps used to be better wines, years ago when they were sent by small boats to Marseilles for shipment to overseas markets.

Languedoc and Roussillon

Q. **Where are Languedoc and Roussillon?**

A. Languedoc and Roussillon may be described as the hinterland of the great inwards curve of the Mediterranean from Provence to the Franco–Spanish frontier of the Pyrenees. This great stretch of country is divided among four Departments: Aude, Hérault, Gard and Pyrénées Orientales. The vineyards of those four Departments are responsible for immense quantities of *ordinaires* wines known as Vins du Midi, as well as small quantities of quality wines. Their acreage and potential productivity are as follow:

	Aude	Hérault	Gard	Pyrénées Orientales
Acres	287,500	425,000	220,000	167,500
Gallons	154,000,000	242,000,000	121,000,000	61,600,000
Quality Wines	5%	0·4%	2·5%	15%

Q. **Which are the quality wines of the Aude?**

A. They are the red wines of Corbières and of the part of the Minervois which is in the Aude Department. The best white wines, still and sparkling, are those of Limoux.

Q. **What kind of wine is made at Limoux?**

A. They make table wines of the *ordinaire* class at Limoux, some 15 miles from Carcassonne, but the wine which they are chiefly known for, in France, is a white sparkling wine called *Blanquette de Limoux*. It is made in the same way as sparkling Champagne is made, and the Limoux people claim that there was sparkling wine made at Limoux long before they had any in Champagne.

Q. **Is there any likelihood that it was so?**

A. It may well have been. There never was any sparkling wine before there were stoppers made of cork clamped on each bottle to keep the carbonic acid gas safely in the bottle, and as Limoux is so near the Pyrenees, where cork-oaks grow, the people of Limoux had a better chance than the Champenois to get corks and to make the first sparkling wine.

Q. **Where is Languedoc?**

A. Languedoc is one of the largest of the old Provinces of France: it stretched roughly from the Lower Rhône Valley in the east to the Upper Garonne Valley, above Toulouse, in the west; and from the Forez to the Mediterranean, from north to south. Practically the whole of the three largest wine-producing Departments – Gard, Hérault, and Aude - also part of the Tarn, are in the former

Languedoc Province, and they produce more but no better wines than any of the other vineyards of France. Most of their wines are of the *ordinaire* class commonly known – and not too favourably known – as *Vins du Midi*.

Q. **Are there any quality wines made in Languedoc?**

A. Of course there are some good Languedoc wines, some table wines like those of Tavel in the Gard, and of Gaillac, in the Tarn; others are sweet dessert wines, the best-known of them being those of Lunel and Frontignan.

Q. **Where is Gaillac?**

A. Gaillac is 14 miles from Albi and 35 miles from Toulouse, on the river Tarn. Its vineyards produce a great quantity and also quite a variety of wines, still and sparkling. The best wines of Gaillac, red, white and *rosés*, are made from Jauzac grapes grown in the vineyards on the left of the river Tarn: they have body, bouquet and breed.

Q. **Where is Lunel?**

A. Lunel is about 15 miles north-west of Montpellier, in the Hérault Department. *Muscat de Lunel* is an *Appellation contrôlée* given to wines made from Muscat grapes grown in the vineyards of Lunel, Lunel-Viel, and Verorgues, and when their alcoholic strength is not inferior to 15°. They vary, in colour, from golden to tawny, and they acquire, with age, a peculiar quality commonly known as *rancio*.

Q. **Is there an English name for Rancio?**

A. There is no English equivalent, although rancid and *rancio* have the same root. *Rancio* may be said to mean what 'high' means when applied to game, and just as there are people who love game when 'high' whilst others loathe the smell of it, there are people who love and others who detest *rancio*, whilst all agree that what some call its *bouquet* and others call its stink is a guarantee of old age.

Q. **Where is Frontignan?**

A. Frontignan is about 12 miles south-west of Montpellier, on the road to Sète, and in the Hérault Department. The wine that bears its name is made exclusively from Muscat grapes grown in the *Commune* of Frontignan or in the adjoining *Commune* of Vi-la-Gardiolle, and its alcoholic strength must not be inferior to 15°. Like Lunel, Frontignan is a sweet dessert wine, tawny in colour, but, unlike Lunel, Frontignan did enjoy a measure of popularity, in England, during the first half of the nineteenth century.

Q. **Where is Roussillon?**
A. Roussillon is one of the southernmost of the old Provinces of France, much smaller than Languedoc: it is wedged between Languedoc and the Pyrenees, north to south, and the Mediterranean sea and the Comté de Foix, east to west. There are vineyards practically everywhere in Roussillon, but those which are responsible for quality wines are those of three valleys: (1) Vallée du Tech, where Banyuls, Picardan, and Collioures wines come from; (2) Vallée du Têt, where they make the better red and white table wines of Roussillon; and (3) Vallée de l'Agly with Rivesaltes, Maury, Côte d'Agly. Côtes du Haut-Roussillon wine, which enjoys a high reputation locally, is also made at Limoux.

Q. **Where is Banyuls?**
A. Banyuls is one of the four *Communes*–Cerbère, Port-Vendres, and Collioure are the other three–along the Mediterranean coast from the Spanish frontier to Argelès-sur-Mer, locally known as La Côte Vermeille. There are both red and *rosés* wines made from the vineyards of those four *Communes*, but they must be sold as Grenache: the *Appellation contrôlée* Banyuls is only given to a wine made from white Muscat grapes from the vineyards of those four *Communes*: it is one of the most popular of the Roussillon *Vins doux naturels*, in France.

Q. **Where is Rivesaltes?**
A. Rivesaltes is a picturesque little town 5 miles from Perpignan on the road from Narbonne, surrounded by vineyards upon the lower foothills of the Pyrenees, facing the blue Mediterranean. Their grapes are mostly white Muscats, the others are Malvoisie, and the Rivesaltes quality wine is a sweet dessert wine, unfortified but of fairly high alcoholic strength.

Q. **Where is Maury?**
A. Maury is a village further away from the sea, upon the higher foot-

hills of the Pyrenees. It is surrounded by vineyards with mostly Grenache noir grapes from which they make a sweet red dessert wine, unfortified but not under 15° alcoholic strength.

Q. **What is the wine called Côte d'Agly?**

A. Côte d'Agly is an *Appellation contrôlée* given to *vins doux naturels* made from Muscat, Grenache or Malvoisie grapes from the vineyards of a few *Communes* in the Agly valley, between Rivesaltes to the east, and Maury in the west.

Q. **What are the wines called Côtes du Haut-Roussillon?**

A. Côtes du Haut-Roussillon is an *Appellation contrôlée* given to *vins doux naturels* made from Muscat, Grenache or Malvoisie grapes grown in the vineyards of the highlands behind Argelès and Banyuls, facing the Mediterranean from Perpignan to the Spanish frontier.

Q. **What sort of wine is called Jurançon?**

A. Jurançon is a dessert wine, rich rather than sweet, orange coloured, with a very distinctive and attractive *bouquet* which has something of a truffle quality. It is made from Petit Manseng, Gros Manseng, and Courbu grapes, which are not grown anywhere but in vineyards of Béarn and Bigorre, between Pau and the Spanish frontier. The *Appellation contrôlée* Jurançon is given to none but the best white wines of the vineyards of Jurançon and a few nearby *Communes*.

Q. **What kind of wine is called Irouléguy?**

A. Irouléguy is a rather heady red wine made from vineyards of the Basque country, south of Bayonne and east of Biarritz. It has a distinctive *bouquet* and flavour and enjoys a high reputation locally, but the quantity made is so small that there is none to spare for export.

Q. **Are there any vineyards in Corsica?**

A. There are over 35,000 acres of vineyards in Corsica, most of them in the Cap Corse district.

Q. **Are there any quality wines made in Corsica?**

A. Very few, maybe 0·1% of the 5,000,000 gallons of beverage wines produced on an average every year in Corsica. The best are the red and the white wines of Vescovato. They also make in Corsica some sweet dessert wines and an *apéritif* marketed under the name of Cap Corse.

ITALY

Q. **Does Italy produce more wine than any other country?**
A. Italy has produced more wine than any other country and may do so again — that is, if and when the French vineyards have suffered from late spring frosts or bad summer weather; otherwise France is the largest wine-producing country in the world and Italy the second.

Q. **Where are the vineyards of Italy?**
A. They are everywhere: on the mainland and the islands, on mountain slopes, plains and valleys, in gardens and orchards, from the Swiss Alps in the north to the islet of Pantellaria in the Mediterranean.

Q. **Of what types are the wines of Italy?**
A. There are many different types of Italian wines but as in all the great wine-producing lands, if not even more than in France, Spain and Portugal, by far the greatest proportion of Italian wines is made up of *ordinaires*, beverage wines, both red and white, honest and rough wines fit for the honest thirst of rough people who have neither the taste nor the wish, let alone the means, for anything better. There is also in Italy a greater quantity than elsewhere of very sweet wines both still and sparkling made in all parts of the country: they appeal to young and old alike, and many of those sweet wines are within the means of all but the really poor.

Q. **Are there any really great wines made in Italy?**
A. No, there are no wines made in Italy comparable to a Trockenbeerenauslese Steinberger, a Romanée Conti or any of the great Châteaux of the Médoç of a good vintage — that is, the really great wines which are in a class by themselves. But there are many very *good*

wines made in Italy, as good as their peers in France or Germany.

Q. **Where do the best wines of Italy come from?**

A. The vineyards of northern and central Italy are responsible for a greater quantity of wines of quality, but there are a few fine, and more fair, wines to be found practically in every part of the country, if only one knows where to look for them. Let us start with the North.

Val d'Aosta

Q. **What vineyards are there in the Val d'Aosta?**

A. There are vineyards right up to the highest altitude at which grapes will grow, at Morgex, 1,000 feet above Aosta, nearly 3,000 feet above sea level. The white wine, known as *Blanc de Morgex*, is a light wine, both in colour and body, with more often 8° than 10° of alcohol. At Chambave, however, they make a very good white wine from Moscato grapes: it is deep gold in colour with 15° of alcohol; it is sold as *Chambave*. The best red wine is from Nebbiolo grapes from Donnaz vineyards and it is sold as *Donnaz*. There are two other red beverage wines of the same alcoholic strength as the Donnaz (12°) but not so well bred; one is from the vineyards of Arvier and is called *Enfer*; the other is from St. Pierre vineyards and is called *Toretta*; both are made from *petit rouge* grapes. There are also two rather pleasant white dessert wines made in the Val d'Aosta, the *Malvasia di Nus* and the *Passito della Val d'Aosta*.

Piedmont

Q. **In what part of Piedmont are the best vineyards?**

A. There are in Piedmont six Provinces and there are vineyards in all of them; but there are only three which are famous for their wines: Turin, where more and better Vermouth is made than anywhere else in Italy; Asti, where more sparkling wine is made than anywhere else in Italy; and Cuneo, where more and better red table wines are made than anywhere else in Italy, Tuscany excepted. The other three provinces of Novara, Vercelli in the North, and Alessandria in the South, have many vineyards, but none of like repute.

Q. **Is Vermouth a wine?**

A. Of course it is. It is a white wine made mostly from Muscat grapes from the Monferrato vineyards. In spite of wormwood, bitter orange, cardamom and other highly flavoured substances used to give Vermouth its peculiar twang and its appetite-provoking quality, it is basically a wine and its degree of sweetness or dryness depends upon the technique used by different firms for their different brands. Their standard brand is usually sold under the name of the House without any qualifying "dry" or "sweet": it is usually medium sweet, with about 15° alcohol, and rather dark in colour. The dry Vermouths are lighter in colour and as a rule of appreciably higher alcoholic strength, hence also dearer since they are liable to a higher duty in foreign markets.

Q. **Which Italian Vermouths are most widely known in England?**

A. The Vermouths shipped by Martini & Rossi, Cinzano, Gancia, Carpano, Cora & Mirafiore, Brega & Rossi.

Q. **Are there any good table wines made in the Province of Turin?**

A. There are just a few, the best being the red wine of Carema, which is sold under that name; it is made from Nebbiolo grapes and its strength is from 12° to 13°. There is also a red table wine made from Nebbiolo grapes at Cesnola in the parish of Settimo Vittone, but it has less body than *Carema*. At Caluso, they make a golden wine from the Erbaluce grape; it is sold under that name together with the indication *secco* or *dolce*, since it is made sweet (*dolce*) as a dessert wine, or not so sweet (*secco*), which is sometimes served as an *apéritif*. As to its alcoholic strength, *Caluso* is never below 12° and the best usually is 15°. In Baldissero, Chieri, Montaldo and Pavarolo they make a slightly sparkling *rosé* wine from Cari grapes which is called *Cari*. It is of low strength and served with fruit or dessert.

Q. **Which is the most famous wine of the Province of Asti?**

A. It is, of course, its sparkling wine, the *Asti spumante*, also known as *Moscato d'Asti* and *Moscato spumante*, all being wines made from Moscato grapes and of very low alcoholic strength (6° or 7°). There is another sparkling *Asti* which is made from Cortese grapes, is paler in colour and of higher alcoholic strength (10° to 11°); it is sold as *Cortese d'Asti*.

Q. **Is Asti like Champagne?**

A. No. The carbonic acid gas in *Asti spumante* and in Champagne is the same, but all else is different. There is in most Asti wines greater sweetness but less alcohol than in Champagne and there is in all of them a Muscat flavour of which there is no trace in Champagne.

Q. **Is not Asti made in the same way as Champagne?**

A. The best brands of *Asti spumante* are made by the *Méthode Champenoise,* that is the same technique of bottle fermentation as practised in Champagne, whilst the cheaper brands are made by the Charmat or *Cuve close* technique of bulk fermentation.

Q. **What differences does it make to the wine?**

A. The difference is that of hand-made and machine made; the first costs more but has a better finish, the other is cheaper but not so nice. The gas produced by fermentation in a bottle is an integral part of the wine, whereas that which has been produced by bulk fermentation in a tank is added to the wine when the wine is bottled, and will leave it as soon as the wine is poured out in a glass.

Q. **Are there any other wines made in the Province of Asti?**

A. Yes, there are quite a number of table wines, mostly red, made from vineyards within the limits of the Province of Asti. They are sold under the name of the grapes from which they were made and to which they owe their chief characteristics, such as *Freisa d'Asti, Barbera d'Asti, Grignolino d'Asti, Brachetto d'Asti* and *Bonardo d'Asti.*

Q. **Is all Asti Spumante made from grapes grown near Asti?**

A. No. There are no less than 44 *Communi* or parishes, the vineyards of which produce wine entitled to the name of Asti.

Q. **Is the Province of Cuneo noted for any quality wines?**

A. Indeed it is. The long stretch of vineyards along the Monferrato Hills is one of the finest in the whole of Italy, and they bring forth every year a considerable quantity of very good red table wines, none better nor better-known than the wines of Barolo and Barbaresco.

Q. **Is Barolo the name of a place or a grape?**

A. Barolo is the name of a place, west of Alba, and it is also the name of a red table wine made from Nebbiolo grapes grown in the vineyards of the parish of Barolo or in the vineyards of six other parishes nearby. The alcoholic strength of genuine Barolo must not be below 13°; it is often 15°.

Q. Is the Nebbiolo Grape the only one grown in the Barolo vineyards?

A. No. The Nebbiolo is a grape which never can have too much sun and it would be useless to plant it in any vineyard not facing due south, whereas other grapes, such as the Freisa, Grignolino and Barbera, may be planted in the vineyards of the same district which are not so favourably sited. They will ripen and make fair enough wines, but not up to the Barolo standard.

Q. Is Barbaresco also the name of a place?

A. Yes, Barbaresco is a place a little nearer to the east of Alba than Barolo is to the west. It is also the name of the red table wine made from Nebbiolo grapes grown in the vineyards of Barbaresco and the adjoining parishes.

Q. Is Barbaresco the equal of Barolo?

A. Not quite. It is lighter in alcoholic strength than Barolo, despite an obvious family likeness, but Barolo is generally considered the better wine of the two.

Q. What is Fontanafredda?

A. It is a model winery, an *Azienda viti-vinicola*, in the Alba district, founded in 1878. It stands on the site of a former royal hunting lodge in a forest which has now been replaced by some very extensive and beautifully kept vineyards, the property of one of Italy's oldest and richest banks.

Q. Are there any other wines made in the Province of Cuneo?

A. Yes, quite a number, mostly wines of the *ordinaire* class which are sold under the name of the grape from which they were made, as well as the name of the village or district of the vineyards, such as *Nebbiolo d'Alba, Nebbiolo di Canale, Nebbiolo di Castellinaldo, Dolcetto delle Langhe, Freisa delle Langhe, Moscato di Cuneo,* and so on.

Q. **Are there any outstanding wines made in the Province of Alessandria?**

A. There are no wines of outstanding quality made in the Province of Alessandria, but there are many table wines and dessert wines made from the vineyards of this Province which are of fair enough quality and most of them are inexpensive. One enterprising vintner markets a white wine made from Cortese white grapes in two grades of quality, one being sold as *Castel Tagliolo* (10° to 11°) and the other as *Castel Tagliolo Superiore* (12° to 13°).

Q. **Are there any quality wines made in the Province of Vercelli?**

A. Just a few red table wines made from Nebbiolo grapes in the vineyards of Gattinara and Lessona (12° to 14°). There is also a red wine known as *Messolone* (13° to 14°) which is made from 75% Nebbiolo and 25% Bonarda grapes from the vineyards of Meisola in the parish of Brusnengo; also a lighter red wine and a *rosé* wine called *Rosso rubino del Viverone* and *Chiaretto del Viverone*, from the vineyards of Cavaglia.

Q. **Are there any quality wines made from the Province of Novara?**

A. Very few. There is a white wine of Barengo (12° to 14°) and there are a few red table wines, one called *Boca* (12° to 13°) from Santuario di Boca; one called *Ronco del Frato* (12·5°) from the vineyards of Ghemme, which is made from Bonardo grapes; also another from the same vineyards but made from Nebbiolo grapes and sold under the name of *Ghemme* (11° to 13°). Lastly a bright ruby wine called *Sizzano* (12° to 14°) which is made from mixed red grapes.

Liguria

Q. **Where is Liguria?**

A. Liguria is the stretch of mountainous country that faces the Mare Ligure or Gulf of Genoa, from the French frontier at Menton to La Spezia.

Q. **Are there many vineyards in Liguria?**

A. There are vineyards practically everywhere, some in terraces cut in the face of rocky mountains that rise almost perpendicularly from the sea, others in the narrow valleys which waters from the

Apennines have cut in the course of ages as they rushed to the sea.

Q. **Are there any quality wines made in Liguria?**

A. There are some but not many. The *Moscatello* of Ventimiglia, a sweet and low-strength Muscat white wine (7° to 8°) can hardly be called a quality wine, and the *Piematore rosso, rosato* and *bianco* of the Bordighera Hills are quite ordinary red, *rosés* and white wines. There is, however, a very nice white table wine made of Rossese grapes from vineyards between Ventimiglia and Bordighera, the best being that which is made near Dolceacqua: it is sold under that name. Another pleasant white wine is made in the northern part of Liguria or Imperia Province: it is made from another white grape, the Vermentino, and it is sold under the name of Vermentino di Imperia (12° to 13°). Farther south, in the Province of Genoa, there are some white table wines of fair quality made from the vineyards of the Upper Petronio Valley at Monasca (12° to 13°) and, in the Lower Petronio Valley at Verice (12°). Another white wine which enjoys a local reputation is the *Polcevera* (11° to 12°) from the Val Polcevera. But farther south, beyond La Spezia, there is a white wine made from the Cinqueterre vineyards that was praised by Pliny nearly two thousand years ago and has been sung about by many poets since then, from Petrarch to D'Annunzio. There is but little Cinqueterre wine made now but that which is made from over-ripe grapes and given a chance to mellow with age is truly a connoisseur's wine. Mention should also be made of a rather remarkable Ligurian wine, the *Campochiesa bianco* (10° to 11°) which is made from Pigato grapes in the Province of Savona, and of the *Vino bianco di Calice* (11° to 13°) which is made from Rossese bianco, Vermentino and Lomassina grapes in the neighbourhood of Calice Ligure, where they also make a pink and a sweet wine: *Rossese rosato* and *Rossese passito*. In the same district Pietra Ligure is reputed for its white *Vermentino* (11° to 12°) and Ortovero for its *Pigato* wines, one sort dry (11° to 12°) and the other sweet (12° to 14°).

Lombardy

Q. **Is there much wine made in Lombardy?**

A. There is a great deal of wine made in Lombardy, some of it of quite good quality but none of outstanding excellence.

Q. **Which are the best wines of Lombardy?**

A. They are the red wines made wholly or mostly from Nebbiolo grapes grown in the Sondrio vineyards of the Province of Valtellina: they are sold as *Valtellina rosso* (10° to 11°), or else *Grumello* (13°), *Inferno* (12°) or *Sassella* (12° to 13°). There are also some white Valtellina wines, mostly sold as either *Valtellina bianco* or *Fracia bianco*, pleasant enough on a hot day but not up to the standard of the reds.

Q. **Which are the next best wines of Lombardy?**

A. The wines of Lake Garda and the Province of Brescia. Some of these wines are considered to be just as good as those of the Valtellina, wines such as the *Chiaretto del Garda,* also called *Moniga del Garda* (12·5°); the *Vino della Riviera* or *Retico* (11° to 12°); *Valtenesi* (11° to 13°) or the *Rosato del Garda*–all better wines than the *ordinaires* of the Brescia hills sold as *Vini rossi dei Colli Bresciani* (9° to 11°). There is, however, one really good white wine of the region; it is made from Torbiano bianco grapes and is known as *Lugana* (11° to 13°).

Q. **Are there no quality wines made in the south of Lombardy?**

A. There are some fair wines made in the southern parts of Lombardy. Near Pavia, the Casteggio Hills are thick with vines and some of their vineyards bring forth wines which enjoy a purely local reputation either because or in spite of the curious names given to them, such as *Frecciarossa di Corteggio* (10°), *Sangue di Juda* (10°), *Buttafuoco* (12°), *Barbacarlo* (11° to 13°). Farther south, between Pavia and Broni, the vineyards of Canneto produce a white table wine—*Canneto Amaro* (12° to 13°) and a white dessert wine, *Canneto dolce* (13° to 14°).

Val d'Adige

Q. **Where is the Val d'Adige?**

A. Val d'Adige is the name given to the Trentino and Alto Adige, from the Italo-Austrian frontier in the north to the province of Verona in the south. The main valley is that of the Adige river which rushes through Merano (1,000 feet high), Bolzano (800 feet) and Trento (600 feet) on its way to Verona (200 feet), but there are other valleys of the Adige's tributaries as well as lakes in that section of the Tyrol which we call Val d'Adige.

Q. **Are there many vineyards in the Val d'Adige?**

A. There are a very considerable number of vineyards in the Val d'Adige and early Roman historians have recorded that some two thousand years ago the Roman legions, as they pushed their way northwards through the Brenner Pass, not only found grapes growing on the mountain slopes but wine that was kept in wooden containers, something quite new to the Romans who kept their wine in vessels of clay.

Q. **Are the wines of the Val d'Adige made differently?**

A. No, the wines are not made differently but the grapes are grown differently, on trellis arbours from 6 to 7 feet in height, some of them up to 8 feet, instead of tied to stakes or a running wire.

Q. **Which are the best wines of the Val d'Adige?**

A. In the Trentino by far the most popular wine is the *Teroldego,* a red wine made from grapes grown in the district of which Mezzocorona is the centre as well as the home of the important college of Oenology of S. Michele.

Q. **What sort of wine is Teroldego?**

A. It is a stoutish wine but by no means coarse, quite acceptable as a very young wine yet possessing a sufficient backbone of acidity to stand the test of time and to improve greatly with age. It is also a very useful wine for blending and improving lighter red wines, and it is sometimes used for this purpose.

Q. **Is there a similar type of wine in the Province of Bolzano?**

A. No, there is a much greater variety of wines made and marketed by cooperative wineries, as in the Trentino, but also by individual firms who sell not only wines under the name of the grape from which they were made and the name of their native village, but Domaine or Château-bottled wines of chosen vineyards.

Q. **Which are the grapes mostly grown in the Alto Adige?**

A. They are mostly 'noble' grapes, such as Pinot noir, Cabernet and Merlot for the red wines; Pinot blanc, Riesling and Traminer for the white wines; Lagrein and other grapes for the *rosés.*

Q. **Is there not a village of the Alto Adige called Tramin?**

A. Yes, the Austrian name of the village of Termeno is Tramin, and it has given its name to one of the best white grapes chiefly grown in the Rhineland, the Tyrol and Switzerland.

Q. **Which are the villages of the Alto Adige renowned for their wines?**

A. Caldaro is one of the more important and its wines are sold as *Colline di Caldaro* (hillside wines), or *Lago di Caldaro* or *Kelterersee* (lakeside wines); then there are Santa Maddalena, Santa Giustina, Lana Postal half-way between Bolzano and Merano, and many more.

Veneto-Venezia Giulia

Q. **Do the vineyards of Verona produce any outstanding wine?**

A. Yes, their white wine known as *Soave* (10° to 12°) may well be called outstanding. It is made of 80% Garganega grapes and 20% Trebbiano grapes and its total acidity averages 0·6%; a light, well-balanced wine, it owes its popularity to its own very pleasing flavour.

Q. **Are there any quality red wines made in the Province of Verona?**

A. Yes, there are some good red table wines made from the vineyards upon the last foothills of the Lessini Mountains, such as the *Bardolino* (10°), *Valpolicella* (11° to 12°), *Valpantena* (11·5° to 12·5°). Among the large number of *ordinaires* red wines sold as *Rossi delle Colline Veronesi* one may chance to come across some very palatable and very inexpensive young wines. They also make, in the Province of Verona, a sweet dessert wine called *Recioto*, both red and white; but the white, *Recioto bianco* (13° to 14°) is much the better of the two.

Q. **Are there any quality wines made in the Province of Vicenza?**

A. Very few. There is a near-Soave white wine which is quite acceptable when the real Soave is not available, and there is at least one quite good red wine which is sold under the name of its native village and of its grape: *Breganze rosso Cabernet* (12°). Most of the Vicenza wines are sold as *Vino rosso* or *bianco dei Colli Berici* (11°) and sometimes under the name of whichever had been the hill of the wine's native vineyard, such as *Arengnano, Barbarano, Brendola, Costozza* or *Orgiano*.

Q. **Are there any quality wines made in the Province of Treviso?**
A. None, but there are nevertheless a number of fair enough table wines made from some of the vineyards of the *Colli Trevigiani,* some still and others sparkling.

Q. **Is there any quality wine made in the far north vineyards of Italy?**
A. Yes, there is some good wine made in what used to be the Duchy of Friuli, now partly in Venezia, Udine and Gorizia. The best is the white wine sold as *Tocai friulani di Lison,* the *Tocai* being the same as the *Pinot Gris* of Alsace. The best red wines are the *Merlot* and the *Cabernet di Friuli,* and the best dessert wine is the *Malvasia di Friuli.* There is also a dessert wine of real merit made in the Udine Province which is called *Piccolit*: its alcoholic strength is 14° and its acidity merely 0·4%. In Gorizia the only wine of note is the *Bianco del Collio,* which is made from grapes grown in San Fiorano del Collio: its alcoholic strength is usually 11°.

Emilia and Romagna

Q. **Are there any quality wines made in Emilia and Romagna?**
A. None, but there are of course a number of table wines which are pleasant enough and some of them even enjoy locally the reputation of being fine wines. Such are the *Rosso del Bosco* (11° to 12°) of Ferrara; the *Lambrusco di Sorbara* (11°) of Modena; the *Lambrusco Grappa rosso* (10°) and the *Sangiovese* (11° to 13°) of Bologna; the *Barbera di Langhirano* (11°) of Parma; and the *Sangiovese di Romagna* (11° to 13°) of Forli and Predappio. The nicest of the white wines – both sweet and *secco* – is the *Albana di Romagna* (12·5°) of Forli, Bertinoro and Cesena.

Tuscany

Q. **Which is the most famous wine of Tuscany?**
A. Chianti is better known in the British Isles and throughout the whole of the civilised world than any of the many other wines of Italy. It has been known in England under that name for a relatively short time but the red wines of the Tuscan hills were known to

Shakespeare, to the Stuarts and the first four Georges as Florence wine which was bottled, as some of it is still bottled today, in straw-covered flasks of thin glass called *fiaschi* (plural) or *fiasco* (singular).

Q. **Is a fiasco as big as or bigger than the ordinary wine bottle?**
A. It is much bigger than the reputed quart or ordinary wine bottle of 75 or 80 centilitres or 6 to the gallon; it holds 2 litres, that is nearly as much as three ordinary wine bottles, but the Chianti that is sold in England is mostly in the half size or *mezzo-fiasco*.

Q. **Is all Chianti sold in straw-covered fiaschi?**
A. No: there is Chianti sold in the usual Bordeaux bottle and there is red wine sold in *fiaschi* which has no right to the name of Chianti.

Q. **How can one be sure to get genuine Chianti?**
A. By buying any of the wines which bear the official Italian *Appellations contrôlées: Chianti classico, Chianti Colli Aretini, Chianti Colli Fiorentini, Chianti Colli Senesi, Chianti Colline Pisane, Chianti Montalbano, Chianti Ruffina or Brolio*. Practically all the Chianti exported bears the brand of the first of those *Appellations, Chianti classico*.

Q. **How can one tell a Chianti classico?**
A. By the *Marco Gallo* which every bottle or *fiasco* of Chianti must bear: it is a black cock in a field of gold and the mark can only be used if the wine has been made from the grapes of a limited number of vineyards along the Via Chiantigiana, the old road that turns and twists as it worms its way over the rocky and wooded Tuscan hills from Florence to Siena.

Q. **What about Brolio?**
A. The Castello di Brolio is the home of Baron Ricasoli who has done more than anybody else in modern times to raise the standard of viticulture and wine-making in Tuscany.

Q. **Is all Chianti red?**
A. Most Chianti is red, but there is also a white Chianti.

Q. **Are there any other quality wines besides Chianti made in Tuscany?**

A. Yes, there are quite a number, such as the red *Brunello di Montalcino* (13°) and the white *Moscatello di Montalcino* (7° to 8°) from the vineyards of the Siennese hills around the little town of Montalcino; also from the vineyards of the Siennese hills comes the famed red wine known as *Nobile di Montepulciano*; and a white wine from the vineyards of San Gimignano, the *Vernaccia di San Gimignano* (11° to 13°).

Q. **Are there any other quality wines besides the above made in Tuscany?**

A. Yes, there are quite a number of other quality wines made in Tuscany and the Island of Elba, which belongs to Tuscany. The *Montalbano* (11·5° to 13·5°) of Pistoia, for instance, is a red wine very similar to Chianti. There is also a *Montecarlo rosso pistoiese* (13°) and a *Montecarlo bianco pistoiese* (13°), both of them very nice table wines. There is also a good white table wine of Cortona, in the Province of Arezzo, called *Valchiana* for short or *Vergine della Val di Chiana* (11° to 12°); the *Bianco Ugolino* of Livorno (11° to 12°) is a white wine of some merit; and in the island of Elba, there is a very remarkable *Moscato dell 'Elba* (14° to 15°) as well as a popular white *Protanico*, both still and sparkling, and a sweet red *Aleatico Portoferraio* greatly prized locally.

Umbria

Q. **Which is the best and best-known wine of Umbria?**

A. It is, of course, the wine of Orvieto, a charming little old-world town perched atop a cone-like hill entirely clothed in vines. The white wines of Orvieto — since there are two: one *secco*, about as dry as a Graves of Bordeaux, and the other *abboccato*, about as sweet as the average Sauternes — are made from Trebbiano grapes, mostly or wholly, the *Orvieto secco* wine from ripe grapes and the *Orvieto abboccato* from over-ripe ones (11° to 12°).

Q. **Are there any other quality wines besides Orvieto made in Umbria?**

A. Yes, there are a few such as the light *Tever bianco* (9° to 10°) and the red *Vernaccia di Cannara*, both from vineyards of Perugia.

Marche

Q. **Are there any quality wines made in the Marche?**

A. None at all. There are, nevertheless, some very fair wines which enjoy quite a reputation locally, such as the white *Verdicchio dei Castelli di Jesi*, and another white wine *Verdicchio di Matenica* (11° to 13°); also two red wines, the *Montepulciano del Conero* (11° to 13°), and the *Bianchello*, named after the local grape from which it is made.

Lazio

Q. **What is the Lazio?**

A. It is the Italian name of the Latin *Latium*, the Rome territory.

Q. **Are there any vineyards in or near Rome?**

A. There are no vineyards in Rome itself, but there are many at no great distance, upon the half-circle of hills to the south-west of Rome. They produce a great deal of wine of fair enough quality; most of them are sold under the non-committal name of *Vini dei Castelli Romani* but the better ones are given the name of their native hill or village, such as *Colli Albani, Colli Lanuvini* or *Colonna; Frascati* or *Velletri rosso* (12·5°), *Aleatico di Genzano* (12° to 15°) or *Castel San Giorgio* (12°) at Maccarese, where they also make a popular *Moscato di Maccarese* (14° to 15°).

Q. **Are there any quality wines made in the Lazio besides those of the Roman hills?**

A. Yes, there is the famous *Est! Est! Est!* wine of Montefiascone in the Province of Viterbo, a few miles south-west of Orvieto; and a rich dessert wine of the same Province called *Aleatico di Gradoli* (14° to 16°), than which there is no headier wine except the *Aleatico secco di Terracina* (16° to 18°).

Campania

Q. **Are there any quality wines made in Campania?**

A. There are a few quality wines made from the vineyards of the

Campania mainland as well as those of the islands off the Campania coast, Capri, Ischia and Procida.

Q. **Which of those islands produces the best wine?**

A. The island of Capri produces the best white wine and its name is often given to the white wines of the other islands, maybe even of the mainland vineyards. The *Ischia superiore* (11° to 13°) is not unlike some of the *Capri bianco* (12·5°) but the plain *Ischia bianco* or *rosso* (8° to 10°) is not to be recommended.

Q. **Is there not a wine of Campania called Lacrima Christi?**

A. There is such a wine which is mostly made from the vineyards of La Resina and Torre del Greco. There is a *Lacrima Christi bianco* (12°) and a *rosso* (11° to 12°); they also make a *Lacrima Christi rosato* and a sparkling *Lacrima Christi* in or near Turin.

Q. **Did not the classical Falernian wine come from Campania?**

A. There is a wine made along the coastline of northern Campania, near Mondragone, and on the lower slopes of Mount Massico, which is called *Falerno bianco* (13°) and *rosso* (12° to 13°) — that is white or red Falernum — but it is difficult to imagine that the Falernian sung by the poets of Imperial Rome, centuries ago, was anything like the *Falerno* of today.

Q. **Are there any other quality wines made in Campania?**

A. There are some rather nice white wines made north of Avellino which are known as *Fiano di Avellino* (10° to 12°) and others farther north along the Tufo coast called *Greco di Tufo* (10° to 13°). East of Tufo, along the Upper Calore river, they make a red wine of real merit which is known as *Taurasi* (12° to 13°). There are vineyards on both banks of the river Volturno, in the Province of Benevento; they produce a great deal of undistinguished table wine, the best of which are the *Solopaca bianco* (12°) and *rosso* (11° to 13°).

Apulia

Q. **Is there any quality wine made in Apulia?**

A. There is no wine made in Apulia which may be rightly called wine of fine quality; but there are some very nice wines, quite good enough for most occasions, such as the *Sansevero* (11·5° to 12·5°), the name given to a white wine from the vineyards north of Foggia. There are also the red, white and *rosés* wines from the Murgia Highlands, farther south, known as *Castel del Monte bianco, rosso* or *rosato* (11° to 12°). In the Cerignola region, from Andria to Bitonto, they make a great deal of very plain wine and a few better ones called *Torre Giulia di Cerignola* (12° to 13°) and *Santo Stefano di Cerignola* (12° to 13°). Still farther south, in the Itria Valley, they make a rather nice white wine called *Bianco di Martina Franca* (11° to 12°). They also make in Apulia a few quite good dessert wines such as the *Moscato di Trani* (16° to 18°), the *Malvasia di Brindisi* (13·5° to 14°) and an aromatic *Aleatico di Puglie*. In the adjoining territory of Lucania there are vineyards upon the lower slopes of the extinct volcano Mount Vulture which produce a red wine of fair quality called *Aglianico del Vulture* (12° to 14°) and some dessert wines greatly prized locally, more particularly the *Malvasia del Vulture* (11° to 16°) and the *Moscato del Vulture* (11° to 15°).

Calabria

Q. **Are there any quality wines made in Calabria?**
A. Yes, there are just a few table wines and dessert wines of merit, such as the *Greco di Gerace* (16° to 17°), the *Pollino di Castrovillari* (13°), the *Giro di Calabria* (15°) and the sweet *Moscato di Cosenza* (15° to 16°).

Sicily

Q. **Which is the best known wine of Sicily?**
A. Marsala is not only the best known wine of Sicily; it is the only wine of Sicily at all known in England and the United States.

Q. **Is Marsala like Port or Sherry?**
A. Marsala is unlike both Port and Sherry although it is, like them, a fortified wine; but it is made differently and from entirely different grapes – the Cataratto and Ingolia grapes mostly. The soil and sub-soil of the Marsala vineyards are also of very different geological

formation and it is their mineral salts that give to the wine its characteristic flavour. Marsala is a fully fermented wine, which means that there is none of the original grape sugar or sweetness left in it when Brandy is added to raise its alcoholic strength from about 15° to 19° or 20°. Then it is that the wine is sweetened and coloured in any way that may be considered suitable to secure a range of wines that will conform to the type and standard of the various 'marks' or brands which the shippers offer to the wine-merchants of England and elsewhere through their agents.

Q. **What is used to colour and sweeten Marsala?**
A. Grape juice which has been brought up by heat to the consistency of a syrup and has acquired in the process the colour of caramel.

Q. **Are there any good table wines made in Sicily?**
A. Yes, there are a number of table wines which are not great but quite good, such as the *Mamertino* (15° to 17°) from Messina Province; the *Eloro bianco* and *rosso* (13° to 16°); and the *Corvo rosso* (13°) from the Syracuse Province.

Q. **Are there any dessert wines besides Marsala made in Sicily?**
A. Yes, there are quite a number, such as the *Corvo di Casteldaccia* (13°); the *Moscato di Noto* (14° to 16°), *Moscato di Siracusa* (16°), *Frappato di Vittoria*, a red dessert wine; and from the islands off the Sicilian shores, the *Moscato di Pantellaria* (15°) and the *Malvasia di Lipari* (14° to 16°), chiefly from the island of Salina, and a little from the islet of Stromboli

Sardinia

Q. **Are there many vineyards in Sardinia?**
A. There are some 150,000 acres of vineyards in Sardinia, 90,000 acres in the southern Province of Cagliari, 33,000 acres in the northern Province of Sassari, and 27,000 acres in the central Province of Nuoro. Their average annual yield is 29 million gallons of wine.

Q. **Which are the most popular wines of Sardinia?**
A. The most popular wines of Sardinia are the *ordinaires*, the cheapest

beverage wines, the alcoholic strength of which is appreciably higher than that of the same type of wine in most wine-producing countries: the common red wine is the *Trebbiano sardo* (12° to 13°); the white, the *Barbera sardo* (13° to 15°).

Q. **Which is considered the best wine of Sardinia?**

A. In Sardinia they consider their *Vernaccia di Oristano* (15° to 16°) the best but it is not particularly different from many other Italian wines made from the same Vernaccia grape.

Q. **Is there a typically Sardinian wine?**

A. There are typically Sardinian *vins de pays* made in small quantities in different parts of the island, the best of them being, probably, a dry white wine with a very distinctive, rather peculiar but attractive bouquet which is made from grapes from some of the many Cagliari vineyards, grapes known locally as *Nuragus,* which is also the name of the wine.

Q. **Are there any other wines enjoying some local reputation?**

A. There are quite a few such as the *Sangiovese sardo* (13° to 14°), *Malvasia di Cagliari* (16° to 17°), *Giro di Sardegna* (15° to 16°) *Monica di Sardegna* (16° to 18°), and *Moscato di Campidano* (14° to 16°).

SPAIN

Q. **Are there many vineyards in Spain?**

A. Indeed, there are more vineyards in Spain than in any other European country, France and Italy excepted. There are over 4 million acres of vineyards in Spain and they are capable of producing in an average good vintage no less than 500 million gallons of wine.

Q. **Where are most of the vineyards of Spain?**

A. There are vineyards in most parts of Spain but more than half of them are on the high plateau of Central Spain in Old and New Castile, Aragon, Leon and Estremadura. About a third of the total are those of the Mediterranean seaboard, from Barcelona to Gibraltar, and westwards from Cadiz to the Portuguese frontier. Last as regards quantity but by no means least as regards the quality of their wines, there are the vineyards of the Ebro Valley in the northwest and those of the Atlantic Provinces, where the summer's heat is not as fierce as it is in Central Spain. Here is a tentative distribution of the vineyards of Spain in those three main categories:

		Acres (approx.)	Gallons (average)
CENTRAL SPAIN			
Castile		1,440,000	168,416,000
Aragon		320,000	21,972,000
Leon		307,000	23,759,000
Estremadura		194,000	26,962,000
	Totals	2,261,000	241,109,000
MEDITERRANEAN			
Levant		810,000	58,441,000
Catalonia and Balearic Isles		500,000	92,922,000
Andalucia		282,000	31,445,000
	Totals	1,592,000	182,808,000
ATLANTIC			
Rioja		187,000	40,301,000
Galicia		94,000	43,542,000
Basque Provinces		14,000	3,663,000
Asturias		4,000	708,000
Canaries		20,000	635,000
	Totals	319,000	88,849,000
	Grand Totals	4,172,000	512,766,000

Q. **What sorts of wine do they make in Spain?**

A. They make all sorts of wine in Spain, mostly quite plain or *ordinaires* table wines, as in every other wine-producing country–some 487 million gallons per year, on an average, out of a total of 512 million gallons. They also make, of course, some quality table wine, maybe some 9½ million gallons per year, but the world-wide famous wine of Spain has been since the sixteenth century, and still is, its Sherry – one of the truly great wines of the world and typically Spanish. Sherry and the other fortified wines of Spain account for nearly 9 million gallons of the annual total production.

Q. **Where do the quality table wines of Spain come from?**
A. Mostly from La Rioja; some from Valdepeñas and some from Valladolid.

Q. **Where is La Rioja?**
A. La Rioja is not legally within strictly defined boundaries. It is the name given to some 30 miles of the Upper Ebro Valley, roughly from Haro to Logroño, about 300 miles before the Ebro reaches the Mediterranean. There are vineyards upon both sides of the river, here and there, mostly on the slopes of treeless hills, among a number of villages, large and small, such as Ollauri, Villabuena, El Ciego, Fuenmayor, and others.

Q. **Do some of the Rioja vineyards produce better wines than others?**
A. There are Rioja vineyards which produce not only better wines than others but different types of wine, as different as Bordeaux is from red Burgundy and Chablis from Sauternes, but they are all sold as Rioja wines – often, however, with some guiding notice such as *Cepa Chablis* or *Cepa Sauterne,* which are offered to the British public by wine-merchants or in restaurants as *Spanish Chablis* and *Spanish Sauterne.*

Q. **Is the quality of Rioja wines due to the grapes or the soil?**
A. The grapes are the same as those grown in many other Spanish vineyards, free bearing species grafted on phylloxera-resisting stocks. The soil is mostly rich and deep and helps to produce large quantities. More suitable soil for grapes likely to make better wines is to be found elsewhere in Spain, where the wines are not nearly of the Rioja standard.

Q. **Is the climate exceptionally favourable?**
A. The climate is more favourable than in most other parts of Spain where the heat is much more fierce during the summer months

than in La Rioja. The chief factor responsible for the fine quality of most Rioja wines is the human factor. Unlike many parts of Spain where wine is made without care or skill, the *vignerons* and the vintners of La Rioja take great pride in the reputation of their wines, and they do their best not to lose it.

Q. **Must Rioja wines be drunk as soon as possible?**
A. Not at all. Both the better Rioja red and white wines, but more particularly the red, improve with age in spite of the fact that the red lose some of their colour and the white get darker.

Q. **Are there any Rioja vintages?**
A. No. Many a bottle of Rioja wine bears a date label which might be easily mistaken for the date of the vintage, but it has no connection with it: it may be the date when the firm was founded or that of the year when the head of the firm was married. Take no notice of it.

Q. **Which are the better known vintners or shippers of La Rioja?**
A. Marques de Riscal, Marques de Murrieta, Frederico Paternina, Bodegas Bilbainas, Gomez Cruzado, Bodegas Francos-Españoles, and Compania Vinicola del Norte de España.

Q. **Are the wines of Valdepeñas anything like the Rioja wines?**
A. Not at all. Both the red and the white wines of Valdepeñas, in the La Mancha Province, are wines of very much higher alcoholic strength – big wines, maybe bigger wines than any other table wine, and yet wines which are best when young. They are evidently not sufficiently well-balanced to stand the test of age.

Q. **Do they not make in Galicia the same type of wine as Valdepeñas?**
A. No. They do make in Galicia some full-bodied red wines of high alcoholic strength but with a touch of acetic acid which is the birth certificate carried by all the *vinos gallegos* or Galician wines.

Q. **Where do the wines of Galicia come from?**
A. Ribadavia is the chief centre of the Galicia wine trade, and the red wines of Leira are said to be somewhat like the *Vinhos verdes* of Portugal. The best white wines are those of Bordones, not far from Sangrego, a fashionable resort. The best is that which is made from

Albarino white grapes and it is chiefly used for making sparkling wines (known as *Spanish Champagne*, in Spain, but nowhere else).

Q. **Is there much sparkling wine made in Spain?**

A. According to official statistics, there were 142,000 gallons of sparkling wines made in Spain in 1955 but there have been greater quantities of this type of wine made every year since then.

Q. **What are the local wines of Valladolid?**

A. One is a very dark red wine sometimes called *bull's blood*: it comes from vineyards between Valladolid and the Portuguese border, a stretch known as *Tierra del vino* to distinguish it from its neighbour called *Tierra del pan*.

Q. **Any white wines?**

A. Yes, the best known of them all is the Rueda, a stoutish golden wine of very fair quality but no better than the little-known wines of La Seca and Nava del Rey in the same district.

Q. **Are there other table wines of fair quality made in Spain?**

A. Yes, there are quite a number of them. They are made — red, white and *rosé* — in all parts of Spain, like the red Alella and the white Casteli del Remy of Catalonia, the vino del Cuarte or *vin rosé* of Valencia, the *rosé* Yecla or Murcia, and the very sweet white Carinena of Aragon.

Q. **Are there any other sweet wines besides Sherry in Spain?**

A. Sherry is not by nature a sweet wine. There is some sweet Sherry, of course; this is Sherry which has been sweetened. But all Sherries begin by being dry and many remain dry to the end. There are quite a number of sweet wines in Spain which have never been anything but sweet, such as the Malmsey of Sitges, the Piorato of Catalonia, the Peralta of Navarre, and, much better known than any of these, the sweet wines of Alicante and Malaga.

Q. **Where is Alicante?**

A. Alicante is a port in a great and beautiful bay, south of Valencia, on the Mediterranean, with a half-circle of mountains behind it. The *Tintilla* is a black grape which is grown almost exclusively in the vineyards of Alicante and it produces a sweet dessert wine which was at·one time quite as popular as Port, in England, under the name of Tent, the anglicised form of *Tinto*, or red.

Q. **Where is Malaga?**
A. Malaga is an old Moorish port and city, farther south than Alicante, huddled below a jumble of mountain. The vineyards of Malaga produce a great quantity of dried raisins as well as much wine, the best of which is made from Pedro Ximenez grapes – a very sweet dessert wine which used to be popular in England during the last quarter of the eighteenth century and the first half of the nineteenth, under the name of Mountain.

Q. **Is there not a Spanish wine called Mistellas?**
A. They make a large quantity of Mistellas in Spain but it is not a wine to drink. It is a kind of wine basis made from fresh ripe grapes like any other wine, but the fermentation of their sweet juice is checked at a very early stage. This partly fermented grape juice is used to make Vermouth, a number of *apéritifs* and cordials and also, sometimes, some imitation wines.

Q. **Do they make any wine in the island of Majorca?**
A. They make mostly table wines, white chiefly, but also some red and some *rosés* wines, *ordinaires* but pleasant enough and very reasonably priced.

Q. **What sort of wine do they make in the Canary Islands?**
A. They make a dessert wine from Malvasia grapes which is somewhat like a Malmsey Madeira not of the finest quality; and yet there was a time, a long time ago, when Ben Jonson and Shakespeare praised Canary Sack as the finest wine in the world.

Sherry

Q. **What is Sherry?**
A. Sherry is fortified wine which is made from quality white grapes, mostly Palomino grapes, grown in the vineyards of Jerez-de-la-Frontera, in the southernmost part of Andalucia. They cover some

15,000 acres roughly between the two rivers Guadalete and Guadal-
quivir during their final run before they reach the sea, the first at
Port St. Mary, at the top end of the Bay of Cadiz, and the second by
San Lucar de Barrameda. The word Sherry is the anglicised form
of Jerez.

Q. **Where is Jerez?**
A. Jerez-de-la-Frontera, or Jerez for short, was for a long time the last
stronghold of the Moors in Spain: they called it Scheriz, nearer even
than 'Jerez' to the English 'Sherry'. It stands on a knoll upon the
high road from Seville to Cadiz, some 9 miles north of Port St. Mary
and 12 miles east of San Lucar. Today Jerez is a very busy and
modern city, the hub of the Sherry trade.

Q. **Can Sherry be made anywhere else?**
A. No. There are wines made in other parts of the world which look
more or less like Sherry and are sold, in Great Britain but not in
Spain, as Sherry — qualified, however, with the name of their country
of origin, either Australia, South Africa, Cyprus, etc. They are all
more or less different from the genuine Sherry, the Sherry of Jerez.

Q. **Does this mean that no wine other than Jerez wine has a right to
the name of Sherry?**
A. It does mean that no wine other than the wine of Jerez has any
moral right to the name of Sherry, even should it be made from
Palomino grapes and in the same way as real Sherry is made. It is
in the soil of the Jerez vineyards that the roots of the Palomino and
other grapes get the minerals responsible for the character of the
wine, just as the Pinot grapes find in the soil of Champagne the
minerals responsible for the fact that real Champagne will always
be different from the hundreds of other sparkling wines made by
the *méthode champenoise*, or Champagne technique.

Q. **What is the soil of the Jerez vineyards made of?**
A. It is made up mostly of lime, clay and sand, but in widely differing
proportions, mixed differently and peppered in a most erratic
fashion with small quantities of various minerals, the importance
of which, as regards their influence upon the eventual character of
the wine, cannot be overestimated.

116

Q. **Are some of the Jerez vineyards better than others?**

A. There are many differences of soil and aspect which are responsible for differences in the quality of the wine made from different vineyards. The best are the richest in lime and are called *Albariza*: they are the vineyards upon which the ancient reputation of Sherry was built and still stands. Macharnudo, Carrascal, Balbaina and Añina are the largest and among the best of the *Albariza* vineyards.

Q. **Is Sherry sold under the name of its native vineyards and vintages?**

A. No. Sherry is made in such a way that it is the 'type' of the wine that matters most, more than the name of the vineyard or vineyards which produced the grapes. As to the vintage, its date is never given nowadays because all Sherries are blends of wines of one and the same 'type' but of different years.

Q. **How is Sherry made?**

A. Sherry is made from white grapes of different species, some sweeter than others–the Pedro Ximenez the sweetest of them all–some commoner than others, such as the Canocaza and the Molla.

Q. **Why grow the commoner species of grapes?**

A. Because they are better suited to the soil of the vineyards chosen for them, vineyards called *Arenas* because their soil is practically all sand, and they are not the sort of grapes that would be suitable for the vineyards called *Albariza*, where the soil is practically all lime, which happens to suit the aristocratic Palomino grapes. It is the same in Burgundy where noble Pinots and common Gamay grapes bring forth wines that differ in quality but are all genuine Burgundy.

Q. **Are the grapes pressed as soon as they are ripe and picked?**

A. No. In September when the Palomino, Pedro Ximenez and other 'quality' grapes are ripe–the commoner sorts ripen rather later–the pickers are out in the vineyards from dawn to dusk. They go up and down the rows of vines unhurriedly and incessantly but not just to pick the bunches of grapes from each vine: they 'take their pick', look at each bunch and cut off none but those which are fully ripe. The others can wait and will be picked later. When a picker has filled the basket which he carries, he comes to the roadside and empties it into one of the two large holders on each side of a patient mule, and when those two large holders are as full of grapes as they can be they are delivered at the farm or home of whomsoever owns the grapes or is acting for their owner.

Q. **And then are they pressed?**

A. Not yet. All the bunches of grapes are laid upon some round esparto grass mats alongside any of the walls of the farm buildings that face south. Palomino grapes are usually left there, sunbathing, for twenty-four hours; but the Pedro Ximenez grapes may be left for as long as a fortnight, being covered up, however, every night with esparto grass matting as a protection from the early morning dew. Then, and only then, are the grapes brought to the *lagar*.

Q. **What is a lagar?**

A. A *lagar* is a rectangular wooden trough, 12 feet square and about 2 feet deep, with a 6-foot iron screw in the centre. Its floor rests upon four legs about 3 feet high. It has a lip to which is attached a funnel for the sweet juice of the grapes to flow into a cask below. A pressing normally consists of 1,500 pounds of grapes evenly spread upon the floor of the *lagar* and dusted over with 3 or 4 pounds of *yeso* or gypsum. At midnight the *pisadores* or treaders, usually four stalwart men, step on the *lagar*. They are shod with shoes studded with projecting nails and they start goose-stepping solemnly and rhythmically, up and down, crushing underfoot the grapes in the *lagar* until day-break, when they go to bed–not always sober but always exhausted. The mass of trodden grape-pulp which is left in the *lagar* by that time is heaped up around the iron screw in the centre of the *lagar* and it is held together by a broad esparto grass tape. The lid of the press is then brought down and forced as far as it will go, squeezing out of the wet grape-pulp most of the grape juice remaining after the night's treading. Even then there is still a little juice left and it is finally crushed out in a hydraulic press; but it is poor stuff and it does not ever get a chance to become Sherry, the quality of which is jealously guarded.

Q. **What happens to the grape juice when it leaves the lagar?**

A. It is sent in casks to the Bodega of the firm which owns the grapes that were pressed or which has bought them from the *vignerons* or farmers.

Q. **What is a Bodega?**

A. A Bodega is more than just a cellar or a warehouse: it is the complete set of offices, cellarage, storage, cooperage and outbuildings which a Sherry shipper needs to make and store his stock of Sherries, as well as generally speaking, conducting his firm's business.

Q. **What happens to the grape juice when it reaches the Bodega?**

A. It soon starts fermenting rather violently and it casts off, at the bung-hole of the cask, dirt and dust and all sorts of 'undesirables' in the form of an ugly scum. Thus does grape juice become wine, new wine –very new, of course, but wine–although not yet by a long way Sherry. Presently a thin film of yeast forms on top of the wine and protects it from the outside air and whatever may be floating on it. Under this *Flor*, as the yeast-film is called, the wine goes on fermenting slowly and in its own way, so that eventually the wine in each cask is found to possess different characteristics of its own. It is then that expert tasters decide, after careful tastings, what is the type of the wine in each of the casks and chalk on the cask a conventional sign corresponding to each of the chief different types, such as *Palma*, for wines which show outstanding distinction; *Palo cortado*, when the wine shows more muscle than breed; and *Rayas* for the stouter wines. All wines at that stage are racked –that is, drawn from their original casks, off their lees–into clean casks and transferred to the *criaderas* or nurseries where all wines of the same type are kept together. At this stage the wines are usually given a first taste of brandy, about 4 gallons per butt, which checks any further fermentation. The next move is the *Solera*.

Q. **What is a Solera?**

A. The *Solera* is the typically Jerez method of building up types of wines that will be true to pattern year after year, a very remarkable and ingenious way of blending wine. All the wines of one and the same *criadera*, that is of the same type, are stacked in tiers, the oldest on the floor level and the youngest on top. To make his blends of Sherry, the Sherry shipper draws as much as he requires from casks of the bottom row and fills them up again from the casks immediately above with the same quantity of wine; the same is done until the topmost butt is used to replenish the cask immediately under it. The wines of the different *Soleras* are to the Sherry shipper what the colours on his palette are to the artist, and he uses them to make up his various types of Sherries, be they *finos, amontillados, olorosos,* and the rest.

Q. **What is a Fino?**

A. *Fino* is one of the most popular of all Jerez wines or Sherries: it is made from a *Palma Solera* — pale in colour, dry, yet by no means acid, with greater grace than power, a *Fino* is the ideal preprandial or *apéritif* Sherry.

Q. **What is Montilla?**

A. *Montilla* is a very dry Sherry, austere and intensely clean on the palate, a wine which, strange to say, is no Jerez wine at all. It is made from grapes grown in vineyards of the Montilla Mountains, in the Cordoba Province, about 100 miles from Jerez. Although, strictly speaking, *Montilla* is not entitled to the name of Sherry, one of the most outstanding of the Jerez wines, *Amontillado*, is named after it.

Q. **What is Amontillado?**

A. *Amontillado* is, or ought to be, a Sherry of the *Fino* type but with greater strength and more colour than most *Finos* — that is, more akin to the wines of Montilla.

Q. **What are the Vinos de Pasto?**

A. They are table wines which vary greatly in quality and style. As a rule they are less dry than *Finos* and they lack their breed, but they are acceptable as beverage wines especially to partner shellfish.

Q. **What are the Olorosos?**

A. They are Sherries usually from *Palo Cortado Soleras*, which vary greatly in style and quality; also in colour, some being golden and others, especially when old, quite brown. They also vary in alcoholic strength from 18% to as much as 24% of alcohol by volume. The lighter *Olorosos* are excellent with soup and the older and stouter ones as dessert wines.

Q. **What are Amorosos and brown Sherries?**

A. They are definitely dessert wines, darker in colour and sweeter than most other Sherries.

Q. **What is Pedro Ximenez?**
A. It is the name of the sweetest of the wine-making grapes grown in Spain, and also the name of a very sweet wine that is made from it.

Q. **What is Vino de Color?**
A. It is no wine that anybody could or would drink, but grape juice boiled to the consistency of a syrup which is used to sweeten some of the less expensive sorts of Sherries.

Q. **What is Manzanilla?**
A. It is the most typical Sherry of the San Lucar de Barrameda vineyards. It is light in colour, of fairly low strength, sharply dry and possessing a rather curious 'finish' which is quite distinctive. It has been described as the sharpness of a green apple but all agree that it is a most refreshing Sherry, equally suitable as an *apéritif* or a table wine, served quite cold, of course.

Q. **What is Pajarete?**
A. *Pajarete* or *Paxarete* is a sweet Sherry made from grapes grown in the Pajarete vineyards between Villamartin and Prado del Rey. It used to be sold in England in Victorian times but its only use today is as a sweetening agent in the making of the less expensive sweet Sherries.

Q. **What is the best Sherry glass?**
A. The best Sherry glass is a glass large enough to hold a fair amount of wine when only half filled. The abortive miniature glasses in which Sherry is served in most public houses and many restaurants are a disgrace and an insult to both the wine and the wine drinker.

Q. **What is a Copita?**
A. A *copita* is a small *copa*, a small glass by Spanish standards; it holds $3\frac{1}{2}$ ounces and it usually is funnel-shaped and flat-footed.

PORTUGAL

Q. **What about Portugal and her wines?**
A. Portugal may be one of the smaller countries of the Continent, yet

her mainland and her island of Madeira rank among the first four wine-producing lands of the world.

Q. **Where are the vineyards of Portugal?**

A. They are practically everywhere but chiefly where the soil is poorest and where no other crop could be raised – from the great granite bluff of the Minho in the north to the sun-baked sea-sand of the Tagus Estuary dunes in the south; and upon the rocky face and foothills of mountains in the valleys of the Douro, Dão and other rivers which have cut their way, in the millenia of prehistoric times, from the highlands of the east to the Atlantic ocean.

Q. **Is such poor soil not a handicap for the vines?**

A. It is a handicap as regards the number and weight of bunches of grapes which each vine is able to bear but, in viticulture as in much else, quantity cannot be had except at the expense of quality – which is why all the better wines of the world are made from grapes grown in poor soil.

Q. **Which are the best wines of Portugal?**

A. Of all the different types of wine made on Portuguese territory – beverage or table wines, dessert wines, sparkling wines – there are two, Port and Madeira, which are more famous, and rightly so, throughout the civilised world than all the other wines of Portugal. They are two of the very few really great wines of the world; they rank with the best wines of Bordeaux, Burgundy and Champagne, the Rhine and the Moselle.

Port

Q. **What is Port?**

A. Port is a wine which is (1) made from grapes grown in the Valley of the Upper Douro; (2) fortified at the time of the vintage; (3) shipped from Oporto. But because all wines entitled to the name of Port must have those 'three dimensions' it does not mean that they are all alike. They are not.

Q. **Which are the principal types of Port?**

A. The chief differences between one Port and another are due in the first place to the quality of the grapes from which each wine is made, and this depends upon the more or less favourable climatic conditions at each vintage—that is the year when the wine was made: this is the same for all wines. Then comes the manner in which the grapes were pressed and the wine 'fortified' in the making; this varies with different wine-makers and it is very important. Thirdly comes the difference due to whether the newly made wine will be bottled early and matured in bottle or else kept in cask and matured in cask—maybe by itself, but as a rule after being blended with other Upper Douro wines: which accounts for the immense variety of types and qualities of Port, i.e., Vintage, Ruby, Tawny and so on. Nor must we forget that there is also some white Port—not lily white, of course, but of a beautiful golden colour.

Q. **Where is Oporto?**
A. Oporto is an ancient city with much charm and character. It is built on a rock and looks down upon the Douro, some three miles before the river reaches the Atlantic at Leixoes. Its business houses and Lodges—or wine stores—are mostly upon the opposite or south bank of the Douro, at Nova Vila de Gaia.

Q. **What is the Oporto 'Factory House'?**
A. The Factory House, at Oporto, is more than a Wine Exchange and a social club: it is the Mecca of all Port-lovers. Its granite house is spacious, cool in the summer and warm in winter; its twin dining-rooms, ballroom and library have dignity and grace; its Chippendale furniture is exquisite; the glass, the silver and all furnishings are perfect; the cellar, of course, is unique.

Q. **Why should Port be made from that part of the Douro called Upper Douro?**
A. Because of the different nature of the soil, and it is from the soil that the roots of the vines get the acids that will give to the grapes the chance to make quality wines.

Q. **Where is the Upper Douro?**
A. The name covers a veritable jumble of mountains from Barca d'Alva, where the Douro enters Portugal from Spain, until it reaches

123

Regua, some 40 miles westwards, where granite replaces schist.
There are vineyards from Regua to San Joao da Foz, where the
Douro flows into the Atlantic; but their grapes can only be used to
make beverage wines, not Port. The vineyards of the Upper Douro
are strictly defined by law and include, besides those cut in the face
of the mountains which form the valley of the Douro, others which
grace the banks of its tributaries. Here, too, the soil derives from
foliated crystalline rock or schist, northward and southward from
the Spanish frontier to Regua. The most important of the Douro
tributaries as regards the acreage of its vineyards is the Corgo.

Q. **Are there famous Châteaux in the Upper Douro as there are in
the Médoc?**

A. There are, but they are called *Quintas*, or Estates. The *Quintas* of
the Upper Douro are mostly large self-supporting Estates and some
of them are immense: Ferreira's *Quinta do Vesuvio*, for instance, on
the left bank of the Douro, where it is joined by the river Teja,
claims seven hills and thirty valleys in its domain. A little further west
there is the *Quinta Roriz*, much smaller but no less famous. Upon
the other side of the Douro there are a number of well-known
Quintas, such as Cockburn's *Quinta da Tua* and Graham's *Quinta
dos Malvedos*; and, further west, two Silva & Cossens *Quintas*,
Zimbro and *Bomfino*, also Offley's *Boa Vista*, Feuerheerd's *La
Rosa*, Da Silva's *Quinta do Noval*, and many others where the best
traditions of wine-making and hospitality are admirably upheld.

Q. **How is Port made?**

A. Port is made in a *lagar*, a square trough made of granite slabs and
from 3 to 4 feet deep. At the time of the vintage, when the grapes
are ripe, they are picked and brought to the *lagar* which is filled
to the top. The grapes are then trodden by bare-legged men, who
link arms and stamp up and down, working in four-hour shifts and
giving the grapes and themselves six hours' rest in between, until
the grapes in the *lagar* look like some kind of runny jam. Soon
after, the thick juice of the crushed grapes begins to ferment and
the man in charge of the *lagar* watches it with the utmost care. As
soon as he thinks it is time to check the fermentation, the liquid con-
tents of the *lagar* are run into a *tonel*, or cask, partly filled with
Brandy, and fermentation stops at once, but by no means for ever.

How much or how little Brandy is to be used has to be decided by the man in charge but, on an average, there are 10 parts of Brandy used to 45 parts of new wine. Presently the new wine is racked from the *tonel* into pipes and sent down to Oporto and Vila Nova do Gaia, to the shippers' Lodges, where it is racked again and usually given a 'refresher' of some 5% more Brandy. It is not Port yet, but the raw material which is to become in time Vintage, Ruby, Tawny, Red or White Port.

Q. **What is vintage Port?**
A. Vintage Port is a wine made from the best grapes of one year or vintage, either from one *Quinta* or Estate or from different vine-yards of the Upper Douro, bottled two years or at most three years from the date of its vintage and given time to mature at peace in a good cellar.

Q. **Is vintage Port better than any other Port?**
A. It is a better wine not only because it is made from none but the best grapes of a good year, but because it possesses a greater measure of personality due to the characteristics of its vintage, and a *bouquet* due to its slow oxidisation in bottle. A good vintage Port is a great wine; all other good Ports are just good Ports.

Q. **What is a late-bottled vintage Port?**
A. It is the wine of one year, a good year of course, matured in wood for some time before being bottled, so that it is ready to drink soon after it has been bottled.

Q. **What is an off-vintage Port?**
A. It is the early bottled wine of a year which was not 'declared' or considered of vintage standard by the majority of Port shippers. It can happen that the grapes of one or a few particularly favoured vineyards turn out much better than the rest, so that the wine made from them is quite of vintage standard. An off-vintage Port may be excellent; it is by no means a second-rate wine.

Q. **How long should vintage Port be kept to be at its best?**
A. Nobody can tell. It depends upon the way the wine was made and kept after it was bottled; also upon the wine-sense of the drinker and

his personal taste. In the good old days of peace and trust, 21 years was considered right for one's boy and his Port to grow up together, and many great Vintage Ports of the past were quite superb when 50 or 60 years old. Today, however, Vintage Ports are mostly bottled in Portugal and made acceptable young to the young.

Q. **What is a vintage-character Port?**
A. It is a red Port, a blend of dark and sweet young wines, which looks rather like vintage Port but lacks the softness and *bouquet* of a vintage Port; it costs accordingly much less.

Q. **What is a Ruby Port?**
A. A Ruby Port is a wine that was 'full purple' — almost black — when first lodged in the cask where it has been kept long enough to lose some of its colour, thus becoming 'Full Ruby', then, a little later, 'Ruby'. It is lighter not only in colour but also in body than vintage Port, but darker than a Tawny Port.

Q. **What is a Tawny Port?**
A. A Tawny Port is a blend of wines kept in cask long enough to lose its original purple colour and acquire the peculiar 'tawny' (orange-cum-red) hue to which it owes its name.

Q. **Is a Tawny Port an inferior kind of Port?**
A. Certainly not. There are as many different sorts of Tawny Ports as there are stars in heaven, and some of them are very beautiful wines, blends of none but fine Ports kept in cask for a great many years. Others, of course, are blends of less remarkable wines and kept for a shorter period; they are not so good and they are not so dear. Yet others are blends of red and white wines of no great age, which cost less and are worth less.

Q. **What is a Crusted Port?**
A. A Crusted Port is a blend of red wines which has been matured in bottle long enough to 'throw a crust' – that is, to have a sediment mostly of mucilage and cream of tartar which should stick to the glass of the bottle as a film which is known as a 'crust'. A bottle of Crusted Port should always be decanted as the 'crust' is liable to slip into the wine when it is served.

Q. **What is a white Port?**

A. A white Port is a wine made like a red Port but with white grapes instead of black grapes. Most white Ports used to be rather sweet and considered a 'ladies wine' but there are white Ports made now which are dry, like Cockburn Dry Tang, and suitable as a pre-prandial wine as a change from Sherry.

Q. **What is a Pipe of Port?**

A. A Pipe of Port is 115 gallons of Port wine in an oak cask known as a Pipe. The vintner who broaches a pipe of Port hopes to fill 56 dozen bottles from the pipe, but he does not always get this full measure owing to occasional leakage or an excessive quantity of sediment or lees.

Q. **How long has Port been popular in England?**

A. For the past two hundred years.

Q. **Was no wine shipped to England from Portugal at an earlier date?**

A. Yes, there were beverage wines shipped from the Minho, the Douro and Lisbon long before they thought of adding Brandy to the new wines-in-the-making, in 1756, and it so happened, by a very fortunate coincidence, that the corkscrew, or bottlescrew as they called it then, was invented in England earlier in the eighteenth century, making it possible to bottle wine in cylindrical bottles safely locked in with a cork driven right home. It made it possible to bottle and bin away the new fortified wines from Portugal and given them a chance to be drinkable after a few years and to become really fine wines when kept a little longer.

Q. **Which are the best vintage years of the twentieth century?**

A. 1908, 1912, 1917, 1920, 1924, 1927, 1931, 1934, 1935, 1942, 1945, 1947, 1948, 1955, 1960.

Q. **Which are the wines of Portugal other than Port?**

A. Portugal produces a great many wines besides Port, a large variety of table wines – red, white and rosés; sweet unfortified and fortified dessert wines; also sparkling wines – from the ordinaires vinhos de Casa to the attractive vinhos verdes and the distinctly luscious vinhos generosos.

Q. **What are the Vinhos de Casa?**

A. They are the wines 'of the house'–that is, the wines which every hotel, restaurant or *pension* in Portugal is obliged, by the law of the land, to give without charge to anybody being served with food, just as in England, whether by law or usage, no caterer can refuse to give water to customers who demand it. Of course, in the more 'Ritzy' hotels of Portugal the rich and the great of this world who patronise them do not know anything about *Vinhos de Casa*, as a rule, but it does happen that one of them, having heard about the wine law of Portugal, will demand some *Vinho de Casa* and his meal; he will be sure of getting sour looks and sour wine. Not so, however, in the many humbler hotels, restaurants and *pensions* of Portugal, where the *Vinhos de Casa*, always red wines, may be quite pleasant, always very young table wines, acceptable as the first wine of the meal, *pour la soif.*

Q. **What are the Vinhos verdes?**

A. They are the best table wines of Portugal, best because they are more typically Portuguese than any of the other wines of Portugal which are made to look and taste as near as possible like some of the well-known French wines, such as Claret and Burgundy, Sauternes and Champagne.

Q. **Are Vinhos verdes green?**

A. They are green in the sense that a freshman is green, pink as his cheeks may be. *Vinhos verdes* are either golden or ruby in colour but they are meant to be drunk when fresh, young and lively.

Q. **Where do the Vinhos verdes come from?**

A. Most *Vinhos verdes* are made from the Azal white grape grown here, there and almost everywhere where there are trees or poles for the vines to climb and attach themselves, north of the Douro and right up to the Spanish frontier–that is, from Peñafiel, about half-way from Oporto to Vila Real, to Viana do Castello and Moncao, in the Minho Province. The juice of grapes grown upon tree-borne vines is richer in acids and poorer in sugar than the juice of grapes from vines that are pruned low, which is why *Vinhos verdes* are so entirely different from all other European wines of commerce. They possess a degree of liveliness entirely their own but their quality and appeal vary greatly according to the degree of skill and integrity of the peasants responsible for them.

Q. **Which are the Vinhos verdes generally accepted as the best?**
A. They are, in alphabetical order, not in order of merit, as follows:
AGULHA, both white and red wines;
ALVARINHA, white wines only;
AMARANTE, both white and red wines;
AVELADA, both white and red wines;
CASA DE CAMPO, both white and red wines;
CASAL GARCIA both white and red wines;
CASAL VINHO, red wine only;
GATAO, both white and red wines;
LAGOSTA, both white and red wines;
MOURA BASTO, both white and red wines.

Q. **Do all Vinhos verdes come from the Minho Province?**
A. Not all of them. There are *Vinhos verdes* made in Lafoes, south of the Douro, west of Pinhel, in the Valley of the Upper Vouga, where the soil is of the same granitic nature as that of the Minho, and where they make wine from the grapes of tree-borne vines.

Q. **Where is Pinhel?**
A. Pinhel is in the Valley of the little Goa river, south of the Upper Douro, shortly after it enters Portugal from Spain. The vineyards of Pinhel produce a variety of table wines but they are chiefly known for their *rosés* wines, the best and the best-known of them being one which is marketed under the name of *Mateus rosé*; it is bottled in a Bocksbeutel-type flagon.

Q. **Which are the vineyards of Portugal responsible for table wines other than Vinhos verdes?**
A. They are scattered in many parts of the country — mostly, as in France and Germany, in the valleys of the rivers, from the Douro and its tributaries in the north to the Tagus and its tributaries in the south, with the rivers Dão and Mondego between them.

Q. **Which are the best table wines of Portugal other than Vinhos verdes?**

A. They are the red wines of Colares and the white wines of Bucellas; next come the Dão wines and those of Aguada, Bairrada, Cartaxo, Alcobaça and the Torres Vedras.

Q. **Where are the Colares vineyards?**
A. They are on the foothills of the Sintra Hills, beyond Estoril, facing the Atlantic. They add up to about 4,500 acres; their soil is of the poorest, all sand, yet the Ramisco grapes manage to find a living in it; they produce on an average 2,000 pipes of red wines every year — wines which are somewhat like some of the red wines of the Rhône Valley.

Q. **Where are the vineyards of Bucellas?**
A. They are further inland than the Colares vineyards, between Sintra and the Tagus, in more sheltered locations where the soil is also somewhat richer. The Arinto grape is the one that is chiefly grown in the Bucellas vineyards and it brings forth white wines which have little *bouquet* but possess a fair body and a charm of their own.

Q. **Where are the Dão vineyards?**
A. They are in the highlands of central Portugal, mostly in the valleys of the Dão and Mondego rivers. The red wines are made from the Tourigo de Dão and the Tinta Pinheira grapes, and the white from the Arinto de Bucellas grapes. They are mostly straightforward, wholesome, satisfying wines which partner perfectly the peasant-type country fare which is so typical of Portugal and so good in Portugal, outside the luxury or fashionable hotels. The same may be said of the wines of Bairrada, between the Bussaco mountains and the Atlantic — Anadia is the chief seat of production; and this applies also to the table wines made south of the Tagus, in the Cartaxo, Alcobaça and Torres Vedras districts. Alcobaça is chiefly noted for its white wines, those of Obidos and Caldas de Rainha being particularly popular. Torres Vedras vineyards bring forth more and better red wines than white.

Q. **Which are the best dessert wines of Portugal?**
A. The best and best-known of the sweet, dessert wines of Portugal is the wine marketed as *Grandjo*; but the chief source of supply is the Setubal Peninsula. The vineyards of the Arrabida mountains

produce a great deal of very popular muscatel wines; the best of them always have a name of their own, such as *Periquita* or *Palmela*.

Q. **What is Carcavelos?**

A. Carcavelos is a fortified dessert wine which was once upon a time quite fashionable in England. It is made from grapes grown near Estoril, where the Tagus Estuary opens out into the Atlantic. It is topaz in colour, with a nutty flavour that is particularly attractive; some is made sweet and some rather dryish.

Q. **Where are the sparkling wines made?**

A. They are made in different parts of the country, but more particularly at Bairrada and Lamego. Some are dry, others are sweet, and all hold in solution the same carbon dioxide as there is in a bottle of sparkling Champagne. All else, however, is different, but whether better or not is just a matter of personal idiosyncracy.

Madeira

Q. **What is Madeira?**

A. Madeira is one of the great wines of the world, a fortified wine made from noble grapes grown upon the terraced slopes of a cluster of hills and mountains on the island of Madeira.

Q. **Is Madeira like Port?**

A. Madeira is quite different from Port, first because it is made from entirely different species of grapes, which give to each type of Madeira its name and its personality; second because Madeira is not made in the same way as Port, but by a method which gives Madeira a much longer expectation of life than Port. It is capable of reaching in old age a higher degree of excellence than any of the other fortified wines.

Q. **Which are the noble grapes from which Madeira is made?**

A. The Malvazia grape must be given first place in point of seniority: it was the first grape to be planted in Madeira early in the fifteenth century by the Portuguese. The wine made from Malvazia grapes has been known in England as Malmsey, and in France as Malvoisie, during some 500 years. It is a sweet dessert wine of fine quality. The grape known as Boal or Bual is responsible for a different type of dessert wine, not so rich as the Malmsey but fuller and more fragrant. Some Madeira is dry almost to the point of austerity and is nowadays mostly made from the Sercial grape. Other species known as Verdelho, Terrantez and Bastardo have practically ceased to be cultivated since the phylloxera invasion of the island in the 1870s.

Q. **Are beverage wines also made from those grapes?**
A. No, beverage wines are made from commoner species of grapes. All of them are of the *ordinaire* class and consumed locally.

Q. **How is Madeira made?**
A. At the vintage time the ripe grapes from many different patches of vines not deserving the name of vineyard are picked by the many peasants (smallholders who grow *primeurs*, French beans, potatoes and tomatoes as well as vines), who sell their grapes to the wine firms of Funchal; these make the wine, keep it and eventually export it. The grapes from different parts of the island are pressed together, but always by separate species, either Malvazia, Boal or Sercial. Their fresh juice ferments and becomes wine — *vinho claro*. The new wine is aged by a stage in a peculiar hot chamber called *estufa*, which it leaves as *vinho estufado* or stoved wine. Some time later it is given a tonic in the shape of some high strength brandy, after which it is entitled to the title of *vinho alcoolisado*, or fortified wine. Now comes the expert blender who makes up a vatting of wines of different vintages but all of the same species of grapes, and his blends become *vinhos generosos* which have to be left to live together and mature in peace before being offered for sale.

Q. **How many acres of vineyard are there in Madeira?**
A. About 42,000 acres.

Q. **How is Madeira sold?**
A. Madeira is sold under the name of the grape from which each sort is made, always with the name of the firm responsible for the quality of the wine, and often under some registered trade mark which is easier for the consumer to memorise and also easier for the shipper of the wine to advertise.

Q. **Which are the best-known Madeira shippers?**

A. In Great Britain these are four British firms: Blandy, Cossart Gordon, Leacock, and Rutherford and Miles.

GERMANY

Q. **Are there many vineyards in Germany?**

A. There are a great many vineyards in Germany, although not nearly as many as there are in France, Italy, Spain and Portugal.

Q. **Where are the vineyards of Germany?**

A. They are practically all in the south-western part of the country, from the Swiss frontier and Baden in the south nearly to Bonn in the north, and from Lorraine and Luxembourg in the west to Württemberg and Saxony in the east.

Q. **Where are the vineyards which produce the best German wines?**

A. They are in what is called the Rhineland – that is, the valley of the Rhine proper, and the valleys of the Rhine's tributaries.

Q. **Are all German wines white wines?**

A. Certainly not. There are many red table wines from German vineyards but almost all of them, like a great many of the plainer white wines, are drunk by the Germans themselves and are not exported.

Q. **Why are they not exported?**

A. Because they are not better than the *ordinaires* or plain beverage wines of the much larger vinelands of Europe and they can be sold in Germany more profitably than in the world's markets at competitive prices.

Q. **Which are the German wines that are exported?**

A. There are many different white wines exported from Germany, some of them from fair to fine in quality and moderately priced; others of superlative excellence, the peers of the greatest white wines of the world and usually more costly than the best of them.

Q. **Why should the best German wines cost so much more than other fine wines of the same standard of excellence?**

A. Because the best German wines possess a higher degree of individuality than most other wines and there are never enough to meet the demand.

Q. **Why should German wines have a greater degree of individuality?**

A. Because they are made differently. In France, and practically everywhere else, the wine that is made from the grapes picked each day is all blended together when the vintage is over, so that all the bottles of wine from the same vineyard and of the same year are the same. Not so in Germany: the wines made from the first to the last pickings of the grapes are kept separately and eventually bottled separately, which accounts for the fact that, at Schloss Johannisberg for instance, they used wax and they now use metal capsules of seven different colours which correspond to different grades of quality of the wine of one and the same vineyard and vintage.

Q. **Does this apply to all German wines?**

A. No, not to all but to a great many among the better-known wines.

Q. **Are those different grades of quality also recorded on the wine's label?**

A. They are, indeed. The native village or Estate of the wine in the bottle is given in larger type than the rest, followed by the name of 'site' or vineyard and preceded by the year of its vintage. Then comes the name of the grapes, usually Riesling. Then may appear one of the following descriptive words according to when and how the grapes were picked:

Auslese, meaning that the grapes were specially selected, sometimes with a qualificative such as *feine*, *feinste*, *hochfeine* — meaning fine and finest;

Spätlese, meaning late-gathered grapes;

Beerenauslese, meaning that none but the best grapes from each bunch were used;

Trockenbeerenauslese, meaning that none but the ripest grapes from each bunch were used;

Stück or *Fuder*, followed by a number, refers to the particular cask in which the wine in the bottle was reared;

Wachstum, Krescenz, Gewächs or *Eigengewächs*, followed by the name of a person or firm or institution, is a record of the vineyard's or site's ownership;

Original Abfüllung or *Abzug*, meaning 'the bottling of . . . ', with the bottler's name added;

Schlossabzug, the equivalent of 'Château-bottled';

Cabinetwein or *Kabinettwein,* the equivalent of *Cuvée réservée,* or Special Reserve;

Naturrein or *Naturwein,* meaning unsugared wine, or not chaptalised.

Q. **Why are the wines of Germany called Hock in English-speaking countries?**

A. Hock is the anglicised name of Hochheim, a small town by the river Main just before it flows into the Rhine opposite Mainz. Its vineyards produce some very fine white wines called 'Hock' for short and the name is also given to the white wines of the Rhinegau, Rhinehesse, the Nahe and the Palatinate, but not to all the wines of Germany.

Q. **How long have some of the wines of Germany been called Hock in England?**

A. Since the early part of the Victorian age. To Queen Anne, to Shakespeare before her and to the Georges after her, all German wines were known as Rhenish.

Q. **Which German wines are not known as Hock?**

A. The wines of the Mosel, Saar and Ruwer are all called Moselle, whilst the wines of Franconia, which are sold in Bocksbeutel flagons, are usually called Stein wines, although the name Stein does not really belong to the wines of Franconia other than those of Würzburg.

Q. **Where do the best wines of Germany come from?**

A. They come from the vineyards of the Rhinegau, Rhinehesse, the Nahe Valley, the Palatinate and Franconia, and from the Mosel, Saar and Ruwer.

Q. **Which are the other wine-producing regions of Germany?**

A. There are ten other regions with *Appellations contrôlées* besides the

135

six which might be called in the 'First Division'. They are Ahr, Baden, Bergstrasse, Bodensee, Grünberg, Lahn, Saale Unstrut, Mittelrhein, Sachsen, Württemberg.

Q. **Do any of those ten regions produce quality wines?**
A. Some of them do. In particularly sunny years there are some very pleasant wines made in the valleys of the Ahr, Lahn and Neckar; also the Mittelrhein region in the north and the Bodensee, or lake region, in the south; but their wines are rarely exported and connoisseurs must go to Germany and look out for them on their native heath.

The Rhinegau

Q. **Where is the Rhinegau?**
A. The Rhinegau is a stretch of land about 20 miles long and from 2 to 5 miles wide from Wiesbaden to Rudesheim, on the right bank of the Rhine, opposite Rhinehesse from Mainz to Bingen. During the Rhine's long run from Switzerland to the North Sea it is only when its northwards course is barred by the Taunus Hills, the back-drop to the Rhinegau, that the great river has to change its course to west and south-by-west until Bingen, when it turns north again. This means that the vineyards of the Rhinegau — some 6,500 acres — are protected by the Taunus from the worst of the weather from the north and east and that, facing as most of them do south and west, they have their full share of whatever sunshine there is.

Q. **Which are the best vineyards of the Rhinegau?**
A. There are three vineyards in the Rhinegau which are so beautifully situated, besides producing wines of such superlative excellence, that they enjoy a worldwide fame greater than that of all other Rhinegau wines: Schloss Johannisberg, Steinberg and Schloss Vollrads. They are also the only three Estates of the Rhinegau each in single ownership.

Q. **In which villages or townships are situated the best Rhinegau vineyards?**
A. In Hochheim, Rauenthal, Erbach, Hattenheim, Winkel, Johannisberg and Rüdesheim.

Q. **Which are the villages or townships with the next best Rhinegau vineyards?**

A. Martinsthal, Walluf, Eltville, Kiedrich, Oestrich, Mittelheim, Hallgarten and Geisenheim.

Q. **Is Hochheim in the Rhinegau?**

A. Geographically speaking it is not, but its wines are so good and so similar to those of the Rhinegau that Hochheim has been voted into the Rhinegau by public acclaim.

Q. **Which are the vineyards responsible for the best wines in each of the villages or townships of the Rhinegau?**

A. Here is a list of those villages or townships with the names of a few, but by no means all, of their good vineyards:
HOCHHEIM. Domdechancy, Rauchloch, Hölle, Kirchestück, Stein, Daubhaus; also Victoriaberg, Falkenberg, Neuberg, Steilweg and Reichestahl.
MARTINSTHAL. Langenberg, Pfaffenberg, Geisberg.
WALLUF. Walkenberg, Mittelberg, Unterberg.
ELTVILLE. Schloss Eltz, Sonnenberg, Langenstück, Sangrub, Taubenberg, Kalbpflicht, Klümbchen, Monchhanach.
RAUENTHAL. Baiken, Gehrn, Wülfen, Rothenberg, Wieshell, Burggraben, Pfaffenberg, Herberg.
KIEDRICH. Gräfenberg, Sandgrub, Wasserose.
ERBACH. Marcobrunn, a vineyard parts of which are owned by different owners, one of whom is Prince Heinrich of Prussia who sells his Marcobrunn wine under the label of Schloss Rheinhatshausener Erbacher Markobrunn, with a red label for the less remarkable wine, a blue label for the better ones and a white label for the best. Other good vineyards of Erbach are Siegelsberg, Honigberg, Hohenrain, Seelgass, Rheinhell, Brühl, etc.
HATTENHEIM. Steinberg, the property of the Prussian Domains, is the finest vineyard; its grapes are pressed and their wine is cared for until ready for sale in the nearby Kloster Eberbach, 2½ miles up country from Hattenheim. Other good vineyards of Hattenheim are Nussbrunnen, Wisselbrunn, Mannberg, Willborn, Engelmannsberg and Hassel.
OESTRICH. Doosberg, Lenchen, Deez, Klostergarten, Pfaffenpfad, Eiserweg, Kellerberg. Oestrich, with 750 acres, has more vineyards

137

than any of the other townships of the Rhinegau.

MITTELHEIM. Oberberg, Edelmann, Honiberg, Neuberg.

HALLGARTEN. Jungfer, Schönhell, Deutselberg, Rosengarten, Hendelberg.

WINKEL. Schloss Vollrads' vineyards (81 acres) are the largest of any of the privately-owned Rhinegau Estates. They are the property of the Matuschka-Greiffenklau family; they are responsible for some of the greatest of all German wines. They are marketed with a green capsule for the less remarkable, a red capsule for the better ones, a green capsule with a gold band for the 'Kabinett' wines, a rose capsule for the *Auslese* wines and a white capsule for the *Beerenauslese* and *Trockenbeerenauslese* wines. Other good vineyards of Winkel are Jesuitengarten, Hasensprung, Honigberg, Kläuserberg, Dachsberg, Oberberg.

JOHANNISBERG. The Schloss Johannisberg with its wonderful vineyard is the most spectacular showplace of the Rhinegau. The wines of the Schloss are marketed under a number of labels and seals, the less remarkable with a red seal, the better ones with a green seal and the next senior with a pink seal, all three without the mention 'Cabinet' on the label. There are four other qualities which are marketed with the name 'Cabinet' on the label, with either an orange, white, sky-blue or gold seal, according to an ascending scale of quality. Other good vineyards of Johannisberg are Hölle, Mittelhölle, Klaus, Klauser Berg; also Erntebringer, Goldatzel, Hansenberg, Kahlenberg, Vogelsang, etc.

GEISENHEIM. Rothenberg, Katzenloch, Kläuserweg, Fuchsberg, Decker, Marienberg, Hoher Decker, Kosackenberg, Lückerstein, Mäuerchen.

RUDESHEIM. Many of the terraced sites of the 'Berg', such as Rüdesheimer Berg Rottland, Roseneck, Bronnen, Hellpfad, Lay, Schlossberg, Mühlstein, Zollhaus, Burgweg, Dickerstein, Hauptmann, Paares, Stupfenort, are responsible for very much fine wine. Among those vineyards not on the Berg: Bischofsberg, Wilgert, Klosterkiesel, Engerweg, etc., also bring forth fine wines.

Q. **Is there not also a Dorf Johannisberg vineyard?**

A. No, there is no vineyard of that name, but there is a white wine marketed as Dorf Johannisberg, made from Riesling grapes from vineyards belonging to a number of small Johannisberg owners.

Q. **Is there no wine made in or near Worms?**

A. Yes, there is still a famous vineyard at Worms, the vineyard shared by three owners: Langenbach, Valckenberg and Freiherr Heyl zu Herrnsheim. It produces the only wine which may be sold as Liebfrauenstiftswein. Originally, when this vineyard belonged to the Canons of the Cathedral, its wine used to be called Liebfraumilch.

Q. **How do the wines of Rhinehesse compare with the wines of the Rhinegau?**

A. They are somewhat like the red wines of the Graves de Bordeaux compared to the great wines of the Médoc: they are softer, more immediately welcoming, but they have not got the firmness and distinction of the born aristocrat.

Palatinate or Rheinpfalz

Q. **Where is the Palatinate or Rhenish Pfalz?**

A. It is a small border State immediately north of Alsace and east of Lorraine, with Rhinehesse and the Rhine beyond to the west and the Nahe Valley to the north.

Q. **Does the Palatinate produce much wine?**

A. The Palatinate, with nearly 40,000 acres of vineyards, produces more wine than any of the other wine districts of Germany – mostly, however, both red (7,800 acres) and white (31,500 acres) wines of the *ordinaires* type and only about 10% of white wines of superlative excellence.

Q. **Which are the vineyards of the Palatinate which produce the finest wines?**

A. They are the vineyards of Forst, Deidesheim, Ruppertsberg and Wachenheim; also those of Kallstadt, Dürkheim and Königsbach.
FORST. Jesuitengarten, Kirchenstück, Ungeheuer, Ziegler, Langenböhl, Freundstück.
DEIDESHEIM. Kieselberg, Hohenmorgen, Grainhübel, Kalkofen, Dopp, Grain, Leinhöhle, Mühle, Rennpfad, Hofstück, etc.
RUPPERTSBERG. Kreutz, Spiess, Nussbien, Gaisböhl, Reiterpfad, Hofstück, Hoheburg.

WACHENHEIM. Gerümpel, Böhlig, Goldbächel, Altenburg, Hägel, Rehbächel, Luginsland.
KALLSTADT. Kobnert, Kreuz, Steinacker, Nill, Saumagen.
DURKHEIM. Michelsberg, Hochbenn, Spielberg, Hochness.
KONIGSBACH. Rolandsberg, Idig, Satz, Reiterpfad, Bender.

Q. **What are the chief characteristics of the Palatinate wines?**
A. The great Palatinate wines are chiefly remarkable for their luscious sweetness. They are not in the least heavy in spite of being so rich; they also possess a great measure of elegance and breed.

Q. **Are the best Palatinate vineyards large or small?**
A. They are not large and they are all divided among a number of owners, all of whom, bar three, have but very small holdings. Reichgraf von Buhl is the sole proprietor of nearly 200 acres, Dr. Bürklin-Wolf owns 159 acres and Dr. von Bassermann-Jordan 90 acres.

Rhinehesse

Q. **Where is Rhinehesse?**
A. Rhinehesse is the high ground that faces the Rhinegau, with the Rhine as its boundary north and east, from Mainz to Bingen, and the Nahe westwards, with some 34,000 acres of white grapes and some 3,600 acres of black or 'blue' grapes.

Q. **Does Rhinehesse produce a great deal of wine?**
A. Rhinehesse produces on an average 13 million gallons of wine, 80% being quite *ordinaires* wines from Sylvaner grapes. It also produces a comparatively small quantity of very fine wines from Riesling grapes grown exclusively in some half a dozen of the 155 wine-producing localities of Rhinehesse.

Q. **Which is the best known of Rhinehessen wines?**
A. The best known of all Rhinehesse wines, maybe of all German wines in English-speaking countries, is the white wine called Liebfraumilch.

Q. **Where does Liebfraumilch come from?**

A. Anywhere. It can be made, and it is made, anywhere in Rhinehesse. Some Liebfraumilch is, of course, very good wine, but by no means all of it.

Q. **How can one tell the Liebfraumilch that is good?**
A. By the name or brand of the shippers who are responsible for the quality of the wine in the bottle: as good trees bear good fruit, good shippers bear a good name.

Q. **Which are the half-dozen Rhinehesse townships, with their vineyards, which produce the best wines?**
A. NIERSTEIN. Easily the first of all the Rhinehesse wine townships both as regards the quantity and the quality of its wines. Some of the best vineyards of Nierstein are: Rehbach, Hipping, Glöck, Orbel, Floss, Pettental, Heiligenbaum, Fuchsloch, Auflangen, Kehr, Kranzberg, Oelberg.
NACKENHEIM. Rothenberg, Stiel, Engelsberg, Rheinhahl, Fenchelberg.
BODENHEIM. Leistenberg, St. Alban, Silberberg, Westrum, Kahlenberg, Ebersberg.
OPPENHEIM. Kreuz, Herrenberg, Steig, Sackträger, Goldberg, Daubhaus, Kerhweg, Reisekahr, Krötenbrunnen, Zuckerberg.
DIENHEIM. Goldberg, Kröttenbrunnen, Tafelstein, Eselspfad, Falkenberg.
BINGEN. Bingen is at the mouth of the river Nahe, where it joins the Rhine, next to Büdesheim, and the best vineyards at this western end of Rhinehesse are those using both names hyphenated, such as Binger-Büdesheimer, followed by the name of the vineyard – either Scharlachberg, Häusling, Steinkrautsweg or Schnackenberg. Other Binger vineyards are Binger Ohligberg, Mainzserweg, Rosengarten, Schlossberg, etc. Also the Binger-Kempter Rheinberg, Pfarrgarten and Kirchberg.

Nahe

Q. **Where is the Nahe?**
A. The Nahe is a river which rises in the Hunsrück Mountains, the beautifully wooded Highlands immediately behind Bernkastel and

the Moselle Valley; it flows into the Rhine at Bingen, opposite
Rüdesheim.

Q. **Which are the best vineyards of the Nahe Valley?**
A. There are some 11,000 acres of vineyards but only 20% of them pro-
duce wines of fine quality. These are west, north-west and north
of Kreuznach, the chief township of the Nahe.
KREUZNACH. Hinkelstein, Kröttenpfuhl, Kahlenberg, Narren-
kappe, Forst, Mönchberg, Steinweg, Kronenberg, etc.
SCHLOSS BOCKELHEIM. Kupfergrube, Kupferberg, Königsfels,
Königsberg, etc.
NIEDERHAUS. Hermannshohle, Hermannsberg, Rosenheck, etc.
NORHEIM. Kafels, Kirschheck, Hinterfels, etc.
MUNSTER. Pittersberg, Langenberg, etc.
ROXHEIM. Hüttenberg, Höllenpfad, etc.
WINZENHEIM. Rosenheck, Honiberg, etc.
BRETZENHEIM. Vogelsang, Schützenhöll.

Q. **What is the type of the Nahe wines?**
A. They are more like the wines of Rhinehesse than those of the
Rhinegau, with a charm and appeal of their own. The best Nahe
Valley wines of good vintages are the peers of the finest Rhinehesse
wines.

Franconia

Q. **Which is the best wine of Franconia?**
A. The best wine of Franconia is the Steinwein, the white wine from
the best vineyards of the rock upon which Würzburg stands: Stein,
Aussere Leiste, Innere Leiste Neuberg, Abstleiste, Harfe, Ständer-
bühl, Schalksberg and Steinmantel.

Q. **Are not all the wines of Franconia Steinwein?**
A. No, they are not; they are Frankenwein, Franconian but not Stein,
although they are sold in the peculiar Würzburg flagon called
Bocksbeutel.

Q. **Are there many vineyards in Franconia besides those of Würzburg?**

A. There are over one hundred villages and townships in the Valleys of the Main and of the Main's tributaries with a total of 7,000 acres of vineyards; but practically all of them produce none but quite *ordinaires* wines. There are only ten townships, besides Würzburg, with vineyards responsible for less than 10% of all the the wines of Franconia. These produce the only wines of fine quality and are:

ESCHERNDORF. Lump, Eulengrube, Hengsberg, Kirchberg.

IPHOFEN. Julius-Echter-Berg, Kronsberg, Kammer, Burgweg, Kalb.

RANDERSACKER. Pfülben, Hohburg, Teufelskeller, Spielsberg, Marsberg.

ROEDELSEE. Kuchenmeister, Echwanleitr, Schlossberg.

VEITSHOECHHEIM. Wölflein, Neuberg.

SCHLOSS SAALECK. Schlossberg.

HOERSTEIN. Abtsberg.

NORDHEIM. Vögelheim.

FRICKENHAUSEN. Kapellenberg.

CASTELL. Schlossberg.

Q. **Are the Steinwein and other Franconian wines among the great wines of Germany?**

A. They are among the most expensive; the best of them are very fine wines but they have not got the *bouquet* nor the breed of the great Rhinegau wines.

Moselle, Saar, Ruwer.

Q. **Is not the Moselle a French river?**

A. The Moselle rises in France and flows for the greater part of its course through France before crossing Luxembourg and coming to Germany, at Wasserbillig, 7 miles west of Trèves or Trier. From Wasserbillig to Koblenz, where it joins the Rhine, the French Moselle becomes the German Mosel.

Q. **Are there vineyards along the Valley of the Moselle and Mosel?**

A. There are a great many in France, in Luxembourg and in Germany.

Q. **Are all their wines at all similar?**

A. Not in the least. The wines of the French Moselle are never above

143

the *ordinaires* level, yet some of the Luxembourg Moselle wines are of a distinctly better quality; but it is only in Germany that there are Moselle wines of superlative excellence.

Q. **Why should this be?**

A. Because it is only during the last laps of the twisty course of the Moselle that the Riesling grapes find in the soil of some of the vineyards – 6,000 acres out of a total of 22,600 acres – a peculiar kind of slate which is responsible for the greater *finesse* and the unique *bouquet* of all the great wines of the Moselle, Saar and Ruwer.

Q. **What are the Saar and the Ruwer?**

A. They are two small rivers which flow into the Moselle, the first above Trier and the other below. Their best vineyards produce very fine wines which are similar to the best wines of the Moselle proper and they are usually dubbed 'Moselle' in the British Isles and the U.S.A.

Q. **Which are the best wines of the Moselle?**

A. They are some of the wines of the Mittel Mosel, below the Upper Moselle and above the Lower Moselle.

Q. **Which part of the Moselle is the Upper Moselle?**

A. There is no legal definition of the Mittel Mosel but it is usually accepted that the Upper Moselle is the part of the river before it is joined by the Ruwer.

Q. **Is there no good wine made in the Upper Moselle?**

A. There is a little, in particularly good years, from grapes grown near Trier and more particularly from those of the Avelsbach vineyards.

Q. **Which are the vineyards of the Mittel Mosel?**

A. They are vineyards on both banks of the river from Ruwer to Pünderich, in the following order:
LONGUICH. Herrenberg, Kirchberg, etc.
MEHRING. Eisenberg, Johannisberg etc.
DETZEM. Königsberg, Lay, Maximiner Klosterberg.
KLUSSERATH or CLUSSERATH. Bruderschaft, Königsberg.
LEIWEN. Laurentiusberg (part of), Ohligsberg.
TRITTENHEIM. Laurentiusberg (most of), Altärchen, etc.

NEUMAGEN. Kirschenstück, Pfaffenberg, etc.

DHRON. Hofberg, Hengelsberg, etc.

NIEDEREMMEL. Günsterlay, etc.

PIESPORT. Goldtröpfchen, Lay, Falkenberg, Treppchen, etc.

WINTRICH. Geierslay, the property of the Hüsgen-Böcking Estate; Ohligsberg, the property of Baron Schorlemer-Leiser; Geyerskopf, etc.

KESTEN. Herrenberg, Niederberg, Paulinsberg, etc.

BRAUNEBERG. Juffer, Lay, Hausenlaufer, Sonnenuhr, etc.

LIESER. Schlossberg, Niederberg, Kirchberg, etc.

BERNKASTEL-CUES. Twin townships on the right and left of the Moselle. The most famous vineyard of the Moselle probably is the Bernkasteler Doktor: its 13 acres belong mostly to the heirs of Dr. Thanisch and to Messrs. Deinhard of Coblenz. Messrs. Lauenburg also own a small part and sell its wine as Bernkasteler Doktor und Graben. Other Bernkastel vineyards: Badstube, Pfaffenberg, Rosenberg, Schlossberg, Lay, etc.

GRAACH. Josephhofer is the property of Reichgraf von Kessel-stadt and the best-known wine of Graach. Other vineyards: Domp-rost, Abtsberg, Münzlay, etc.

WEHLEN. Sonnenuhr is the most famous vineyard of Wehlen. Other vineyards: Lay, Klosterlay, Rosenberg, etc.

ZELTINGEN. Schlossberg, Himmelreich, Sonnenuhr, Rotlay, etc.

ERDEN. Treppchen, Prälat, Herrenberg, etc.

UERZIG. Würzgarten, Lay, Schwartzlay, etc.

KINHEIM. Eulenlay, etc.

KROEV or CROEV. Niederberg, Paradies, Petersberg, etc. 'Nack-tarsch' is not a vineyard but the registered label of a very popular brand of wine.

WOLF. Goldgrube.

TRABEN-TRARBACH. Twin townships on the left and right of the Mosel. Trarbach, Schlossberg, Ungsberg, Königsberg, etc.

ENKIRCH. Steffensberg, Herrenberg, Battereiberg, etc.

Beyond Enkirch, from Pünderich to Coblenz, there are many wine-producing localities in what is known as the Lower Moselle and 'Krampen', the name given locally to a hairpin bend of the Moselle between Eller and Cochem.

Q. **Which are the wine-producing localities of Krampen?**

A. They are: Beilstein, Briedern, Bruttig, Ediger, Ellenz-Poltersdorf, Eller, Kochem, Meerf, Poltersdorf, Pommern, Senheim, and Valwig.

Q. **Which are the other wine-producing localities of the Lower Moselle?**

A. They are: Aldegund, Alf, Bremm, Briedel, Karden, Klotten, Kobern, Merl, Moselkern, Pünderich, Treis, Winningen, and Zell.

Q. **Are the Lower Moselle wines any good?**

A. In good years—that is, in sunny years—many of the Lower Moselle wines can be quite nice, light and pleasant, not great but good and good value; they are, as a rule, cheaper.

Q. **Which are the best wines of the Saar?**

A. They are the wines of Scharzhofberg, Scharzberg, Braune Kupp and all the vineyards of Wiltingen.

Q. **And which are the next best?**

A. They are:
OBEREMMEL. Agritiusberg, Rosenberg, Scharzberg (part of), Karlsberg, etc.
AYL. Kupp, Neuberg, Herrenberg.
OCKFEN. Bokstein, Geisberg, Herrenberg, Heppenstein.
WAVERN. Herrenberg, Goldberg.
KANZEN or CANZEM. Altenberg, Sonnenberg, Berg, etc.
NIEDERMENNIG. Euchariusberg, Herrenberg, Zuckerberg, etc.
In particularly good vintages the vineyards of Filzen, Saarburg and Serrig also bring forth some quite pleasant white wines.

Q. **Which are the best wines of the Ruwer?**

A. They are the Karthäuserhofberger of Eitelsbach and the Maximin Grünhäuser from the von Schubert Estate.

Q. **Are there any other fine Ruwer wines?**

A. There are a few, the wines of the other vineyards of Eitelsbach and those of Kasel or Casel.

Sparkling Wines

Q. **Do they make sparkling wines in Germany?**
A. Indeed, they do. They make more sparkling wines than they do in Champagne.

Q. **But it is not Champagne?**
A. Of course not. It is either German sparkling wine made from German wine and sold with the name of the place where it was made, or else it is made in Germany from wine imported as still wine from anywhere where cheap white wine may be had and it is sold as *Sekt* with the name or brand of the firm responsible for the bubbles.

Q. **Is it any good?**
A. Some of it is very cleverly made and most Germans love it. There is also quite a demand for both the *Sekt* and sparkling German wines in many of the markets of the world.

Q. **Which are the finest vintages of the twentieth century for German wines?**
A. They are: 1900, 1904, 1905, 1911, 1915, 1917, 1920, 1921, 1929, 1933, 1934, 1935, 1937, 1942, 1943, 1945, 1947, 1948, 1949, 1953, 1955, and 1959.

OTHER WINES OF THE WORLD

Switzerland

Q. **Are there many vineyards in Switzerland?**
A. There are a great many vineyards in Switzerland, in 20 out of the total number of 29 Cantons, but they are very unevenly distributed, many more vineyards being in the Cantons nearest to France than anywhere else.

Q. **What is the average production of wine?**

A.   The average production of Swiss wines is 11,300,000 gallons of white wine and 5,700,000 gallons of red wines, a total of 17,000,000 gallons.

Q.   **What is the quantity of quality wines made in Switzerland?**

A.   All the quality wines of Switzerland are made in what the Swiss Administration knows as *Suisse romande*, that is the Cantons nearest to France; *Suisse orientale*, that is the Cantons nearest to Germany; and *Suisse italienne*, that is the Cantons nearest Italy. The average quantity of quality wines made from the vineyards of those three administrative divisions is as follows:

	White wines (Gallons)	*Red and rosés wines* (Gallons)	*Total* (Gallons)
SUISSE ROMANDE	10,000,000	500,000	10,500,000
SUISSE ORIENTALE	900,000	1,600,000	2,500,000
SUISSE ITALIENNE	26,000	943,000	969,000
	10,926,000	3,043,000	13,969,000

Q.   **Are the Swiss quality wines made from Swiss species of grapes?**

A.   No. They are made from the same grapes which produce quality wines in France and Germany, which are given different Swiss names in different Swiss Cantons. Thus, many of the best Swiss white wines are made from white grapes called Chasselas in France and Gutedel in Germany, but they are called Fendant vert in the western Cantons of Switzerland, and Markgräfler in the eastern Cantons. They also grow in the Cantons of Geneva and Vaud a white grape which they call Fendant roux or Fendant rouge, which is the same as the grape called Roussette or Roussane in nearby Savoie. The white grape which is known in Alsace and in Germany as Sylvaner is called in Switzerland Gros Rhin. As regards red wines, most of the best wines are made from a grape called Dole in Switzerland, but nowhere else; it is a cousin of the Burgundian Gamay. The Burgundian Pinot Noir is also grown, although to a smaller extent, in Switzerland where it is commonly known as Bourgogne or Burgunder.

Q.   **Which are the best wines of the western Cantons?**

A. They are the white wines of Vaud, Valais and Geneva and those of Neuchâtel and the Jura vineyards.

Q. **Which are the best wines of Vaud?**
A. They are the wines of Lavaux, the name of a mountainous semi-circular sweep of vineyards from Lausanne to Montreux, a distance of about 10 miles. Its steep slopes are clothed with vines which produce the greater proportion of the best quality white wines of Switzerland. They face south to the sparkling blue waters of the Lake of Geneva whilst, behind them, rises the formidable mass of the snow-capped Bernese Alps. Lavaux begins at Pully, where vines grew until recently but which is now a suburb of Lausanne. It stretches to Vevey, by way of Cully, Epesses, Villette, Saint Saphorin, Rivaz and other villages, their white houses set like jewels in the emerald of their vines.

Q. **Which is the best wine of Lavaux?**
A. There are a number of white wines which claim to be the best but there are two which are better known than others overseas to wine connoisseurs, more particularly in the United Kingdom and the U.S.A. They are the Johannisberg from Cully, made from Riesling grapes originally brought over from Johannisberg in the Rhinegau: and the Dezaley, which is made from Fendant grapes from vines grown higher up the same slopes.

Q. **Are not the Clos des Abbayes and the Clos des Moines the best wines of Lavaux?**
A. They are the wines of two vineyards which are the property of the City of Lausanne; good wines, of course, but whether better or not than any of the other good wines of Lavaux matters very little, since they are not for sale. They are used exclusively for Municipal hospitality.

Q. **Which are the best wines of the Valais?**
A. They are the white and the red wines of Sion, from vineyards of the lower slopes of the Valais heights; also the much more typically Valaisian wines of the Visp to Zermatt vineyards, 3,600 feet above sea level, the highest of all European vineyards, where they make the *Gletscher* or Glacier wines and also a sweet *Vin de paille* known

as Soleil de Sierre, which is made from Malvazia grapes now and again, when climatic conditions happen to be particularly favourable.

Q. **What is the wine they call Heidenwein?**

A. It is the name of the best white wine they make in the Visp Valley entirely from Traminer grapes, the Swiss name of which is Heiden.

Q. **What about the wines of the Canton of Geneva?**

A. They are mostly light, pleasant enough white wines of the *ordinaire* class, quite acceptable when very young, particularly on a hot summer's day; but they do not compare, as regards quality, with the better wines of Vaud, Valais and Neuchâtel. They are made from vineyards both west and east of Geneva; the first in the Valley of the Rhône, in the short run of the river from the Lake of Geneva to Savoie; the others, which are very much more important, east of Geneva, along two ranges of hills facing the northern shore of the Lake of Geneva. The first and shortest of those two stretches is called La Petite Côte, from Coppet to Nyon, and the other, which is known as La Côte or La Bonne Côte or La Grande Côte, has a greater depth of vineyards and runs from Begoins and Luins eastwards almost as far as Ouchy and Lausanne in Vaud.

Q. **Which are the best wines in the Canton of Neuchâtel?**

A. They are the red wines of Cortaillod and the white wines of the Domaine de Champreveyres, the first being made from Burgunder (Pinot noir beaunois) and the other from Fendant vert (Chasselas) grapes. All the better vineyards of Neuchâtel are on terraces cut ledgewise along the slopes of the heights facing the north-western shore of the Lake of Neuchâtel, near Neuchâtel itself, and at Auvernier, Colombier and Saint-Blaise. They also make *rosés, oeil-de-perdrix*–the peculiar near-tawny colour of a partridge's eye! –and some sparkling wines as well.

Q. **Which are the best wines of the Canton of Berne?**

A. They are the wines of the Lake of Bienne vineyards, which are practically a continuation of the Lake of Neuchâtel vineyards. At Neuville, on the northern shore of the Lake of Bienne, and at Twann, on the opposite shore, they make a white wine–dark gold and of high alcoholic strength–quite different from any other Swiss white wine. The best red wine of Bienne is that which is made at Erlach from vineyards opposite St. Peter's Inseln.

Q. What kind of wine is made in central and eastern Switzerland?

A. Mostly wine of the *ordinaire* class for the ordinary thirst of the ordinary people of the land, chiefly red wine made from Klevner grapes. The best of the red wines come from vineyards alongside the southern shore of the Lake of Zurich around the villages of Herrliberg, Meilen and Erlenbach. Farther east, in the Canton of Schaffhausen, along the valley of the infant Rhine and overlooking Lake Constance and the Black Forest beyond, much of the local red wine is called Hallauer, from the village of Hallau; but there are also some red wines of better quality made from Klevner grapes, such as the Rheinhalder, Herrenberger and Stockarberger. The two wines of Schaffhausen, however, which are reputed the best are the red Osterfinger and the white Siblinger.

Q. What sort of wine is Halbrot?

A. It is a cheap pinkish table wine which is made from grapes of various colours and parentage pressed together.

Q. Is there any wine made in the Canton of Thurgau?

A. There is a little wine made in Thurgau, the only one of them with any claim to quality is the red Karthauser.

Q. What sort of wine do they make in the southern Cantons?

A. Mostly very poor quality wines from *producteurs directs* or ungrafted vines. The vineyards of Ticino, the southernmost and most beautiful Swiss Canton, look quite lovely in the enchanting scenery of Lugano but they do not bring forth any lovely wines. Their best wines are wines made from Merlot grapes: they are not very distinguished but fair enough and, of course, much better than the majority of the Canton's red wines which are made from Isabella and suchlike grapes.

Q. Is there no white wine made in Ticino?

A. There is a little and it is of better quality than the red. It has more body and greater alcoholic strength than most other Swiss white wines.

Q. **Do they make any wine in the Grisons Canton?**

A. They do make a relatively small quantity of red wine from Klevner grapes which are picked late, when fully ripe and sometimes over-ripe. It is very dark, of high alcoholic strength, rather rough when young; but it is the only Swiss wine which repays being kept in casks for 2 or 3 years, and then in bottles for much longer.

Q. **What is the wine they call Completer?**

A. It is the red beverage wine of the Grisons Canton: it enjoys and deserves great reputation locally.

Luxembourg

Q. **Are there many vineyards in Luxembourg?**

A. There are a great many all along the valley of the Moselle, chiefly around the three old cities of Remich, Worlmeldanger and Graven-macher.

Q. **What sort of wine do they make in Luxembourg?**

A. They make some very nice white wines, light, dry, intensely clean on the palate – not unlike some of the quality white wines of Switzer-land. They have little *bouquet* and do not repay keeping for any length of time; but they are very pleasing and attractive when young.

Yugoslavia

Q. **Where is Yugoslavia?**

A. Yugoslavia is the country born on the deathbed of the old Habsburg dynasty after World War I, east of the Tyrolese Alps and of the Adriatic, west of Bulgaria, south of the Danube and north of Albania and Greece.

Q. **Are there many vineyards in Yugoslavia?**

A. There are a great many vineyards in many parts of Yugoslavia, those of Slovenia and Dalmatia being the more important and also producing the better-quality wines.

Q. **Where is Slovenia?**

A. Slovenia stretches from the Tyrolese Alps and Styria, in the west, below Klagenfurt, to Istria southwards and the Dinaric Alps over-looking the gulf of Trieste. Eastwards, Slovenia extends to the Pannonian plain and the Danube, in the north, and to Croatia in the south.

Q. **Where are the chief vineyards of Slovenia?**
A. The chief vineyards of Slovenia may be divided into four different districts:
(a) Lutomer and the Mura river;
(b) Maribor and the Pohorje and Kozjak Mountains;
(c) Bizeljsko, and the Krka and Sava valleys;
(d) The Gorizia Hills, Istria, Brda and the Vipava Valley.

Q. **Which are the best Lutomer wines?**
A. They are the white beverage wines made from Riesling and Sipon (pronounced *sheepon*) white grapes grown on the foothills of the Pohorje Mountains, at the eastern limit of the Kozjak Massif in vineyards facing south and south-east.

Q. **Which are the best wines of Maribor?**
A. They are the fairly sweet white wines made from Muscat and other grapes grown chiefly in vineyards which grace both banks of the River Mura, to the east of Maribor, as well as dry beverage white wines mostly sold under the name of the grapes from which they were made, such as Sylvaner, Riesling and Traminer. At Radgona, in eastern Slovenia, they make some sparkling wines, most of them rather sweet.

Q. **Which are the best wines of Bizeljsko?**
A. They are the red beverage wines and the *rosés* wines which are usually sold under the name of *Cvicek*, of which there are two sorts, one still and the other sparkling. They also make a great number of white wines which are lighter in body than the white wines of Lutomer: they are mostly sold under the name of their grapes, such as Riesling, Sauvignon, Sylvaner or Traminer next to the name Bizeljcan.

Q. **Which are the best wines of Gorizia?**
A. The best wines of Gorizia are the white wines of Brda and the

Gorizia Hills – *Briska belo vino* and *Gorskia belo vino*; the *Zelenec,* which is not unlike the *Vinho verde* of Portugal; and the *Rebula,* a sweet white wine from Brda. Also the white wines of the Vipava (Wippach) Valley which possess a green sheen through their gold which places them in a class quite by themselves. The more popular of the red wines are sold under the name of their grapes – Pinot noir, Cabernet and Merlot mostly; under the red wine of Krast– *Kraski Teran*; and the very dark red wine of *Crni Kal,* in northern Istria.

Q. **Which are the best wines of Dalmatia?**

A. Although there are more vineyards in Dalmatia than in Slovenia, none of the wines of the Dalmatian mainland – mostly red wines – is of the same standard of quality as the wines of Slovenia – mostly white. The islands off the coast of Dalmatia also have their vineyards; one of those islands produced a wine which was shipped to England at the beginning of the nineteenth century: it is the island of Vis, better known as Lissa, its Italian name. Most of the wines now produced in this island are of the *ordinaire* class, not unlike the Schiller-wein of Württemberg and Baden. Its only two quality wines are the *Zlatarica,* a dry beverage wine, and the *Kapljica Goldtröpfchen,* a 'Mark' dessert wine of tawny Port type.

Q. **Which are the other Yugoslavia wines of note?**

A. There are the red and white wines of Korcula, the best red wines being those made from *Cerljenac* grapes and the more *ordinaires* from *Plavac* grapes. All the better white wines are made from two species of vines with small but very sweet grapes, the *Vugava* and the *Rukalac.* One of the best known wines of Korcula is GRK, pronounced Gurk, which is tawny in colour and possesses a curious 'farewell' or after-taste, more thirst-provoking than thirst-quench-ing. The *Dingac* is a popular Korcula wine which looks like any ordinary Claret but has a distinctive almond flavour.

Q. **Is there a Yugoslavia wine known as Prosek?**

A. Yes, it is a *Prosecco rosé* wine, one of the very best of *rosés,* which is made in small quantities from centenarian grapes grown in the island of Bisevo, opposite Komiza, the only vineyards of Yugoslavia that escaped the scourge of the phylloxera.

154

Q. **Do they not make some fine liqueurs in Yugoslavia?**

A. Yes, they have made for many years past at Zara, now called Zadar, the world-renowned Maraschino liqueur, as well as Cherry Brandy. Yugoslavia is also the land of Slivovica, not a liqueur but the best of all Plum Brandies.

Hungary

Q. **Is Hungary one of the important wine-producing countries of Europe?**

A. Hungary is one of the important wine-producing countries of Europe and of the world, not only because its vineyards produce a great deal of wine but because they are responsible for one of the most remarkable and famous of all wines: Tokay.

Q. **Where is Tokay?**

A. Tokay is a market town which was once upon a time of great strategic importance, built as it is at the junction of the two rivers Tissa and Brodrog, on a spur of one of the westernmost buttresses of the Carpathians. It has given its name to that fabulous wine, Tokay, and to the Tokaji-Hegyalja district, some 5 square miles of mountainous country in the north-eastern corner of Hungary, where the Carpathians stand between Hungary and Czechoslovakia. No wine may be given the name 'Tokaji' which has not been made from grapes grown within the officially defined limits of the Tokaji-Hegyalja.

Q. **What kind of wine is Tokay?**

A. Tokay is not a kind of wine but the name of a number of quite different wines ranging from *Tokay Essencia*, of which there is but very little and that little very expensive, to *Tokay Aszu*, which many wine connoisseurs consider the finest of all unfortified dessert wines. There are also *Tokay Szamorodny*, a fine table wine, and some commercial brands of *ordinaires* entitled to the name of Tokay.

Q. **What is Tokay Essence?**

A. *Tokaji Essencia* (Hungary), *Tokay Essenz* (Germany and Austria) and *Tokay Essence* (U.K. and U.S.A.) is a freak wine made differently from any other wine. It is made from over-ripe Furmint white grapes, when the vintage is particularly good. The grapes come from those favoured vineyards upon the slopes above Tokay, facing south and *open* to the wind from east and west.

Q. **Has the wind anything to do in the ripening of the grapes?**

A. No, not in the actual ripening of the grapes but in their remaining sound when over-ripe. Somehow or other when grapes of a *sheltered* south site, protected by a fold of the land, reach the over-ripe stage of the 'noble rot', the rot is by no means so noble and the grapes not so sound.

Q. **Is it not the same as the Trockenbeerenauslese grapes of the Rhineland?**

A. The *Tokay Essence* grapes are specially selected over-ripe Furmint grapes like the *Trockenbeerenauslese* Riesling grapes of the Rhineland but instead of being put in a wine-press, as they are in Germany, they are piled in a cask open at the top and with a hole in its floor or bottom. This cask, packed with over-ripe grapes, is stood upright over a tub into which the very sweet juice of the grapes, that burst under their own weight, drips in slowly but surely and eventually becomes *Tokay Essence,* a wine with little alcohol, sweeter than honey, with a wonderful *bouquet* and flavour. What is so remarkable is that this low-strength concentrate of grape juice will remain perfect, if not for ever certainly longer than any of the fortified wines, Madeira excepted.

Q. **What about Tokay Aszu?**

A. *Tokay Aszu,* or *Ausbruch* (in German), is not a freak wine like *Tokay Essence.* It is a very fine sweet dessert wine made from over-ripe selected Furmint grapes and fermented in the same way as *Trockenbeerenauslese* or Sauternes.

Q. **Is it made like Château Yquem?**

A. Not at all. All bottles of Château Yquem of one and the same vintage bear the same label and contain the same wine, but the bottles of *Tokay Aszu* of one and the same vintage do not bear exactly the same labels and they contain wines of different degree of sweetness, the sweeter being invariably dearer than the others.

Q. **Why is this?**

A. It is because *Tokay Aszu* is made as no wine is made out of Hungary. The casks in which the new wine is kept each hold the wine of one pressing only, which may mean a different wine in each cask since the technique is to add to the wine-in-the-making either 1, 2, or 3 or as many as 6 *puttonyos* of the best *Trockenbeerenauslese* grapes of the Essence standard after being kneaded into a pulp in a trough.

Q. **What are Puttonyos?**

A. A *Puttony* (Pl. *Puttonyos*) is the Hungarian name (*Büttig* in German) of specially made wooden hods which men carry strapped on their backs, full of grapes. When the label on the bottle states '1 *Puttony*' or '1 *Büttig*' it means that the wine in the bottle is sure to be nice and sweet; but if the label says 2, 3, 4, 5 or 6 *Puttonyos*, the wine in the bottle will certainly be sweeter and dearer according to the number of hods of special *Trockenbeerenauslese* grapes that went into the making of the wine.

Q. **What about Szamorodni?**

A. The *Tokay Szamorodni* (*Szamorodner* in German) is a white wine which is made like most white table wines elsewhere. It may be as sweet as most Sauternes if made in a fine sunny year from grapes fully ripe or overripe, and its alcoholic strength may reach 14°. It is a fine dessert wine. But there is also a fairly dry *Tokay Szamorodni*, a table wine of the white Graves de Bordeaux dryness, which is made when the summer has not been so fine and the grapes are not so ripe.

Q. **Are there any other wines made in the Tokay-Hegyalja?**

A. There are many other more *ordinaires* wines made in the district. Some bear a brand name like *Forditas* and *Maslas,* cheaper sweet wines made from the lees of Aszu pressings; some bear a generic name, like *Asztali,* the cheap table wine of the district; others are nameless or known locally by some local name and consumed locally.

Q. **How important is the wine production of the Tokay-Hegyalja district?**

A. The average production of the Tokay-Hegyalja vineyards is 2,650,000 gallons and the proportion of *Tokay Essence* may be put down as 0·05%, *Tokay Aszu* 0·50%, and *Tokay Szamorodni* 3·2%.

Q. **Which are the more important wine-producing districts of Hungary other than Tokay?**

A. There are important vineyards in the regions of the Lake Balaton, Eger, Villany-Pecs and elsewhere.

Q. **Which are the best wines of the Lake Balaton vineyards?**

A. The white wine of Badacsonyi known as *Badacsonyi Keknelu* is considered, in Hungary, as a wine of really fine quality among table wines, whilst the *Badacsonyi Szurke-Baratis* is a more luscious, golden dessert wine: the same wine is also known as *Badacsonyi Auvergnas Gris*. The *Badacsonyi Rizling* is also a popular dry white wine and the best red wine is made from Burgunder red grapes and called *Badacsonyi Burgunder*.

Q. **Which are the best wines of the Eger vineyards?**

A. The best-known wine from the vineyards of Eger, some 120 miles north-west of Budapest, is the *Egri Bikaver,* meaning 'bull's blood' on account of its dark red colour. It is a big, stout but by no means common red wine. Another favourite is the *Debroi Harslevelu,* a fairly sweet wine made from Harslevelu grapes. There is also a good deal of *Leanyka* table wines made from grapes of the Eger vineyards, some being *Szaraz* (dry) and others *Edes* (sweet).

Q. **Which are the best wines of Villany-Pecs?**

A. The vineyards of Villany, in the County of Pecs, in the extreme south-western corner of Hungary, produce some very fair table wines, both red and white. The red is made from Kadarkas grapes and shipped in Bordeaux bottles; the white wine is shipped in Moselle bottles.

Q. **What other quality wines are made in Hungary?**

A. There are a number of other quality wines made in Hungary such as the golden wine made from white Ezerjo grapes from the vineyards of Mor, near Budapest; the pale white table wine made from Riesling grapes at Nezmely, near Mor; the greenish-yellow wine made from Furmint grapes from the vineyards of Somlyo; the *Muskotaly,* made from Muscat grapes, and the *Szilvanyi Zold,* made from Green Sylvaner grapes in several different parts of the country.

Q. **Are there any sparkling wines made in Hungary?**
A. Indeed there are. Quite a number of sparkling wines are made in Hungary, most of them of a high standard of quality.

Austria

Q. **Does Austria produce any remarkable wines?**
A. No, there are no great Austrian wines but there are a number of quite pleasant table wines made from grapes grown in the vine-yards of Niederösterreich, Steiermark and Burgenland.

Q. **Which is the most popular wine of Austria?**
A. The most popular wine of Austria is probably the *Heuriger* or new wine of Grinzing, now a suburb of Vienna; but the *Gumpoldskirchener*, the white wine of Gumpoldskirchen, in Lower Austria, is also very popular locally and a better wine.

Q. **Which is the best white wine of Austria?**
A. The best white wine of Austria is probably the wine of Rust, in Burgenland.

Q. **Which is the best red wine of Austria?**
A. The best red wine of Austria is made from grapes grown in Voslau and Baden, south of Vienna.

Czechoslovakia

Q. **Are there many vineyards in Czechoslovakia?**
A. About 60,000 acres, more than half of them, (37,000 acres) being in Slovakia. They produce on an average 11 million gallons of wine per annum, no less than 80% of which is white. There is a little red, and some production of table grapes.

Q. **Are the wines of Czechoslovakia quality wines?**
A. Many of them are, and all of them are made from the same species of vines as are grown in Germany and Hungary. The culture of American hybrids is prohibited.

Q. **Are the wines of Czechoslovakia made by large firms or small vignerons?**

A. The vineyards are cultivated in 830 different communities by a very large number of small *vignerons* who have to do what they are told by the officials in charge: they pick their grapes when told to pick them, and they deliver them to the State-staffed wineries, where wine is made according to rule. Whilst the wines of Czechoslovakia are never bad, they are never great: they are made with great care and skill; the uniformity of their quality is at the same time their chief asset and responsible for their lack of appeal.

Bulgaria

Q. **Are there many vineyards in Bulgaria?**

A. There have been many vineyards in Bulgaria for centuries, as the climate of the country is ideal for viticulture and there are many parts of the country where the soil is very suitable. In pre-communist times, there were some 4,000,000 peasants who owned small paches of vineyards where they grew grapes and made wine as their fathers had done before them, just enough for themselves.

Q. **What has happened since?**

A. Large blocks of vineyard have been planted under the control of experts in such a way that they can be cultivated by mechanised cultivators in less time and at lower cost. Seven State wineries have also been built in different parts of the country and the grapes grown in the modern large cooperative farms are processed in those wineries, where the equipment is one of the most up-to-date pattern, and the staff highly trained and efficient. So that there is now more and better wine made in Bulgaria than ever before.

Q. **What sort of wine is made in Bulgaria?**

A. Every sort for which there is a demand at home and abroad, table wines, red, white, *rosés*, sparkling wine and fortified wines, all made to rule and to order.

Greece

Q. **Is Greece one of the important wine-producing countries?**

A. Indeed, it is. Greece has been the cradle of the civilisation of the grape, the source of the culture of our wine-drinking Western World. There are today over half a million acres of vineyards in production in Greece.

Q. **Is wine made from all the grapes grown in Greece?**

A. No. There are 333,000 acres, or about 60% of the total, which are planted with various species of wine-making grapes; 158,000 acres with varieties of drying grapes, mostly raisins and currants; and 41,000 acres with dessert grapes.

Q. **Is any part of Greece responsible for a greater production of wine than any of the others?**

A. Yes. The Peloponnese has the greatest acreage of vineyards, and they are responsible for 29% of the total wine production of Greece, as well as for 54% of the total production of currants and sultanas.

Q. **Which are the best wines of the Peloponnese?**

A. They are the Mavrodaphne and the Muscats.

Q. **Are Muscats fortified wines?**

A. They are not.

Q. **Are there different types of Muscats?**

A. Yes, although all have a more or less obvious flavour of the muscat grape, they differ according to the soil of various vineyards and the techniques favoured in different districts: the three most popular Muscats, in Greece, are the Muscat of Patras, the Muscat of Rion, and the Muscat of Aghaia.

Q. **Which are the best table wines of the Peloponnese?**

A. They are the white Mantinia, from Central Peloponnese, and the red Nemea, from the Province of Corinth.

Q. **Is there not wine made in some of the Greek islands?**

A. Indeed. There are vineyards in almost all Greek islands.

Q. **Which is the Greek island with the greatest acreage of vineyards?**

A. It is the island of Crete: its average yearly production is 8,690,000 gallons of red wine and 2,408,000 gallons of white wine.

Q. **Which Greek islands produce the most famous wines?**

A. The wines of the islands of Samos and Lemnos have been praised by poets and others since the days of Homer, and they are still highly esteemed today, but chiefly the Muscats.

Q. **Which are the other popular wines of the Greek islands?**

A. The following would surely qualify for a place among the more popular wines of the Greek islands:
The white wine of the island of Eubea known as Chalkis;
The white wines of Thera, some dry and others sweet;
The red table wines of Paros and Kea;
The red wine of Rhodes;
The 'Santa Mavra' white wine of Leucade;
The red 'Ropa' wine of Corfu.

Q. **Are there no wines made in Macedonia and Thrace?**

A. There are some wines made now in Macedonia and Thrace: their vineyards were completely destroyed by the phylloxera some 50 years ago and they were not replanted until recent years.

Q. **Which is the best wine made in Macedonia and Thrace?**

A. It is the red Noussa made from grapes grown upon the foothills of Mount Velis, some 60 miles north-west of Salonika.

Q. **Is there not a Greek wine called Retsina?**

A. Indeed, there is. It is perhaps the most typically Greek wine.

Q. **What is Retsina's outstanding feature?**

A. Retsina's outstanding feature is its smell and taste of resin.

Q. **How does resin get into Retsina wine?**

A. When the ripe grapes are picked at the vintage time, and crushed, their sweet juice is collected in a cask, tub or tank where it will ferment and become wine, but before this happens, a small quantity of pine-tree resin, about 1% of resin to 99% of grape juice, is added to it; it becomes part of the wine as the grape juice ferments and becomes wine.

Q. **Why is resin added to Retsina wine?**

A. It is done now to keep up an age-long tradition, and because the Greeks have acquired a strange liking for the flavour of resin in their wine.

Q. **When was resin first used in Greek wine?**

A. Nobody knows: it happened so long ago. Some say that resin was used as an antiseptic in times of epidemics; others say that new wine was kept in casks made of fir trees, but all that one can be certain of is that most Greeks, and few others, love Retsina.

Cyprus

Q. **Are there many vineyards in Cyprus?**

A. There are about 100,000 acres of vineyards in Cyprus, mostly in the Limassol district; also in the Paphos district. In 89% of the Cyprus vineyards grapes are grown for the making of wine, brandy, grape juice (sterilised) and raisins; in 6% of the vineyards grapes for the table are grown; in 5% the grapes are newly planted, and have not reached the production age.

Q. **What is the average annual production of the Cyprus vineyards?**

A. The Cyprus annual production is 111,000 tons of grapes as follows: 35,000 tons of grapes for the making of wine, brandy and concentrated grape juice suitable for export;
28,000 tons of dried grapes or raisins, also for export;
4,500 tons of table grapes of high quality, suitable for export;
28,000 tons of grapes for making the more *ordinaires* wines and rough spirit fit only for local consumption;
15,500 tons of grapes eaten in the island as fresh fruit.

Q. **What are the grapes mostly grown in Cyprus?**

A. All the grapes grown in Cyprus are the classical grapes grown in all the wine producing countries of Europe; there are no American hybrids, and, so far, Cyprus is phylloxera-free.

Q. **Which are the wines mostly made in Cyprus?**

A. The Cyprus wineries make red, white and *rosé* dry table wines, some Port type fortified wines and a Malmsey type of wine with a long tradition behind it called Commandaria, but the wines they make in greater quantities and better than most are imitations of different types of Sherry.

Q. **Is wine making a new industry in Cyprus?**

A. The making of Sherries, Brandies, Vermouths, sterilised grape juice and other wines for which there is a demand overseas is modern, but there were grapes grown and wine made in Cyprus for home consumption many centuries ago, long before the birth of Christ and even the birth of the Roman Empire.

Turkey

Q. **Are there many vineyards in Turkey?**

A. Indeed, there are many vineyards in Turkey, nearly 2 million acres, but only from 3% to 3½% of their grapes are used to make wine.

Q. **What happens to most of the grapes?**

A. Some are eaten as fresh fruit, most are dried for raisins and sultanas.

Q. **Where are most of the vineyards of Turkey?**

A. There are grapes growing in most parts of Turkey, but the larger vineyards are in Thrace and the many isles of the sea of Marmara; also in the islands of the Aegean sea; next in importance are the vineyards of central Anatolia, and least are those of south and south-east Anatolia.

Q. **What is the average annual production of wine in Turkey?**

A. The average annual production of wine in Turkey is just under 4,300,000 gallons, 71% white wines, 21% red wines (dry table wines), and 8% dessert wines.

Districts	*Gallons*
Thrace and Marmara	2,200,000
Aegean	990,000

Central Anatolia	1,775,000
South and South Eastern Anatolia	330,000
Total average production per annum	5,295,000

Q. **What is the standard of quality of the wines of Turkey?**

A. Wine is made in Turkey under Government control and guidance from quality grapes – no American hybrids, and the standard of quality is high. The white table wines are on the whole the best; their alcoholic content varies from 11° to 12°; the alcoholic content of the red table wines varies from 12° to 13°, and that of the dessert wines from 16° to 17°.

Q. **Are any of the wines of Turkey exported?**

A. In 1961, there were 220,000 gallons of wine exported from Turkey to Sweden, 150,000 gallons to West Germany, 4,400 gallons to Norway, and 1,120 gallons to the United Kingdom.

Lebanon

Q. **Are there vineyards in Lebanon?**

A. There are 58,000 acres of vineyards in Lebanon, but 1,137 acres only are planted in wine-making grapes.

Q. **Where are the Lebanese wine-making grapes?**

A. Mostly upon the slopes of Mount Lebanon from 2,000 to 3,300 feet above sea level.

Q. **What is the wine production of Lebanon?**

A. The average annual wine production of Lebanon is 770,000 gallons, 80% red wine.

Q. **Are there any quality wines made in Lebanon?**

A. Yes, there are some very fair wines made from quality grapes with due care and skill, but the majority of the wines are of the *ordinaire* class.

Malta

Q. **Are there any vineyards in Malta?**

A. There have been vineyards in Malta for the past three thousand years, but there are no old vines now because the phylloxera wiped out the old vineyards of the island less than fifty years ago: they have been replanted since with vines grafted on American roots with some of the classical French and Italian grapes.

Q. **What is the importance of the vineyards of Malta?**

A. The vineyards of Malta now cover about 4,000 acres. There are, however, some 9,000 *vignerons*, most of them owning a few vines only. They cannot and do not attempt to make wine but sell their grapes to the island's wineries where grapes of many small vineyards are crushed and processed.

Q. **What type of wine is made in Malta?**

A. Mostly white table wine, some *rosé* and a little red wine, almost exclusively table wines, some of them of better quality than others, none of them costing more than 1s. 6d. to 2s. per bottle in the island's shops, or 5s. per bottle in hotels and restaurants.

Israel

Q. **Are there any vineyards in Israel?**

A. There were grapes in Palestine before there were Jews, and there are vineyards in the modern State of Israel, which is part of Palestine. The best are in the Valley of Sharon and the hills of Samaria.

Q. **What is the average production of the vineyards of Israel?**

A. 26,000 tons of grapes.

Algeria

Q. **Is Algeria one of the largest wine-producing countries in the world?**

A. Algeria produced a very considerable quantity of wine, an average of 300 million gallons per annum up to 1963 when the French, who had civilised the land in 130 years, had to go, swamped by a faster breeding Moslem population. How much longer the vineyards of Algeria will be properly cultivated, and how much longer Algerian wine will receive the loving care and skill it demands, nobody can tell.

Tunisia

Q. **Are there many vineyards in Tunisia?**

A. There are some 135,000 acres of vineyards in Tunisia, of which no less than 115,000 acres are planted in wine-making grapes, and 20,000 acres in table grapes.

Q. **Do any of the Moslem natives own vineyards?**

A. Many Moslem natives own vineyards and grow one-third of the total quantity of grapes produced in Tunisia. Three-fifths of the Tunisian vineyards are owned by natives, most of them own from 5 to 15 acres only, but there are a few who own up to 50 acres.

Q. **Who are the people responsible for the other two-thirds of the Tunisian wine production?**

A. Two-thirds of the Tunisian wine production come from the two-fifths of the Tunisian vineyards owned by French firms with holdings from 50 to 500 acres, their better methods of cultivation and vinification being responsible for the higher figures of production of wine per acre.

Q. **What is the average production of the Tunisian vineyards?**

A. The average production of the Tunisian vineyards is 40 million gallons, of which barely 10% is consumed in Tunisia.

Q. **What happens to 90% of the Tunisian wines?**

A. They are exported, mostly to France but also in increasing quantities to Germany, Holland, Scandinavia and some African countries.

Morocco

Q. **Are there many vineyards in Morocco?**

A. There are no less than 210,000 acres of vineyards in Morocco and their average production of wine is 60 million gallons per annum.

Q. **Where are the chief vineyards of Morocco?**
A. There are more vineyards in the Meknes region than in any other: they produce all kinds of wine, red, white and *rosés* table wines, dessert wines and sparkling wines.

Q. **Which other regions of Morocco produce different kinds of wine?**
A. In the Fez region the best wines are the whites; in the Berkane region, the vineyards produce mostly Muscat grapes and Muscat wines; those of the north and east of Rabat produce mostly big and dark red wines; those of the Casablanca region are best known for their *pelure d'oignon* and *rosés* wines; those of the El Jadida region and of the Damnat region are responsible for the traditional *vins gris* of Morocco, duller in colour than the *rosés* and sharper in taste, reputed to be the most effective thirst-quenchers of all summer drinks.

South Africa

Q. **Are there many vineyards in South Africa?**
A. There are a few vineyards in the Transvaal and some other parts of South Africa which are of little or no commercial importance, but there are very large vineyards, responsible for some 120 million gallons of wine each year, in the Cape Province.

Q. **When were the vineyards of the Cape first planted?**
A. Vines were first planted near Cape Town, at Protea, in 1653, by Johann van Riebeek, and, a few years later by Simon van der Stel, at Constantia, near Wynberg, where wine is still being made today.

Q. **Where are most of the Cape wines made today?**
A. The vineyards of the Cape which produce some of the best table wines are still those of the Cape Peninsula between Table Bay and False Bay, but their acreage is very small compared to that of Paarl, Stellenbosch and the Coastal Belt, stretching from False Bay, in the East, to Wellington, in the West, and as far as the first continuous range of mountains in the north. Lastly, there are the vineyards of

the Little Karoo, widely scattered between the Coastal Belt and the Zwartberg, where the climate is sub-tropical during the summer, and where they grow grapes for drying (raisins and sultanas), as well as for making some dessert wines and brandy.

Q. **What is Paarl?**
A. Paarl is the name given by Johann van Riebeek, in 1659, to a great granite rock marking the gateway to the Cape Peninsula from the Drakenstein Valley and the North. It is also the name of a 'far-flung' town, mostly one unending main street with trees and houses along some seven winding miles of the river Berg. The K.W.V. have their Headquarters at Paarl, and also distilleries, cooperage, and fabulous quantities of brandy maturing in bond.

Q. **What does K.W.V. stand for?**
A. They are the initials of the Ko-operatieve Wijnbouwers Vereeniging van Zuid-Afrika that is the South African Wine Farmers Association, or SAWFA. It is a cooperative Society which groups, guides, and controls nearly the whole of the wine-farmers of the Cape and finds profitable markets for their wines and brandies at home and abroad. It is admitted even by enemies of monopolies that K.W.V. are mainly responsible for the present high standards of quality of the wines of South Africa and for the prosperity of the South African wine farmers.

Q. **How long has K.W.V. functioned?**
A. It was founded by C. W. H. Kohler in 1917 and it has now been functioning successfully during the past 40 years.

Q. **Where is Fransch Hoek?**
A. Fransch Hoek lies at the head of the Drakenstein Valley on the way from Paarl to Stellenbosch. It owes its name to the fact that its first vineyards were planted in the seventeenth century by French Huguenots who had sought asylum in Holland and were shipped to the Cape by the Dutch.

Q. **Where is Stellenbosch?**
A. Stellenbosch is a University town founded in 1679 by Simon van der Stel: it is to the Cape what Montpellier is to French viticulture and

Geisenheim to German viticulture and oenology. It lies 31 miles from Cape Town with flourishing vineyards on all sides.

Q. **Which are the other places of importance in the Coastal Belt?**
A. The three townships of any size west of Stellenbosch are Montagu, Robertson and Worcester, islands in a sea of vines.

Q. **What is called Little Karoo?**
A. Little Karoo is a name given to a tableland about 15 miles wide, crossed from east to west by some parallel mountain ranges, north of the Coastal Belt. Its vineyards lie sheltered in narrow valleys and most of them are irrigated so that they produce a greater quantity of grapes per acre than the other vineyards of the Cape, which depend on local rainfall alone.

Q. **What is the standard of quality of South African wines?**
A. The standard of quality of South African wines is very high as a result of the policy adopted by K.W.V., a policy of quality which they have the means to enforce. But there are also some ambitious and independent wine farmers who attempt with conspicuous success to produce prestige wines of exceptionally high quality. Mr. Bainsfather-Cloete, at Alphen, Constantia is one of them; Mr. Bernard Podlashuk, of Bellingham, Groot Drakenstein, is another, and there are a few more.

Q. **Which is the most popular South African wine?**
A. In the British Isles the most popular South African wine is the South African Sherry: there is one bottle of it sold in Great Britain for every two bottles of the real Sherry from Spain. In South Africa, however, there is a considerable demand for the white table wines of the Cape, commonly called Hock, also Riesling, Steinwein, Johannisburger, and so on; also for the red wines, mostly Shiraz sold in Burgundy bottles. There is also a great demand for *rosés* wines and even for a red fortified wine known as Pontac, which is not exactly a connoisseur's wine but the favourite of the Cape 'gentlemen of colour'.

Australia

Q. **Are there many vineyards in Australia?**

A. There are a great many vineyards in Australia, 132,768 acres in production, in 1962, according to official statistics, when they produced 230,800 tons of wine-making grapes.

Q. **Is not less than 2 tons per acre a very poor yield?**

A. It would be, but these figures are deceptive. A large number of Australian vineyards grow no wine-making grapes at all, but grapes which are eaten as dried grapes, currants, raisins or sultanas.

Q. **Do official statistics tell how much wine was made from 230,800 tons of grapes?**

A. They do: those grapes produced 42,234,994 gallons of wine.

Q. **Are Australians wine-drinkers if they consume such a quantity of wine every year?**

A. The Australians, as a nation, are not wine-drinkers: many drink tea, and soft drinks only; many drink beer and spirits only; but there are more and more every year who drink wine as well, of course, as anything else they happen to fancy at the time.

Q. **What happened then to $1\frac{1}{4}$ million gallons of wine made in one year?**

A. Less than half the total quantity remained wine, i.e., 11,074,598 gallons became fortified wines and 6,903,169 gallons unfortified wines, dry and sweet table or dessert wines as well as some sparkling wines.

Q. **What happened to the rest of the wine?**

A. It was distilled into brandy (5,598,173 gallons) and fortifying spirit (15,291,316 gallons). There were also smaller quantities which became Vermouth, liqueurs, sterilised grape-juice and so on.

Q. **Which are the more popular fortified wines in Australia?**

A. About five-eighths of the Australian fortified wines are wines of various Sherry types, fully half the quantity being of a sweet type and known as 'Sweet Sherry', whilst the other types range from sweet to medium sweet, dry and very dry. The better Australian Sherries are *'Flor'* fermented, as in Spain, and are marketed as Flor Sherries. About two-eighths of the other fortified wines are red wines of the Port types, either 'vintage', 'ruby', 'crusted', 'tawny' and so on. One-eighth of the whole is made up of wines which are marketed as White Port, Madeira, Tokay, and a number of different registered brands.

Q. **Which are the more popular unfortified wines of Australia?**

A. Two-thirds of the unfortified wines of Australia are red table wines chiefly sold under the better known names of their European prototypes such as Burgundy and Claret, often with the name of the grape from which the wine in the bottle was made, such as Hermitage (Shiraz), Cabernet, etc., often also with the name of the wine's native district and always with the name or brand of the firm responsible for the wine. One-third of the Australian unfortified wines are white wines, dry or sweet, mostly dry, which are sold, like the reds, as White Burgundy, Hock, Moselle, Sauterne, etc., with or without the name of their grape — Semillon, Rhine Riesling, etc.–and that of their native district. The sparkling wines, which are mostly white wines — but there are a few red and *rosés* sparkling wines — are mostly sold as Champagne with the name of the wine-maker or his brand. The geographical names of wines are not protected by law in Australia.

Q. **Is Australian sparkling wine made in the same way as Champagne is made in France?**

A. All the better brands of sparkling wines marketed in Australia as Champagne are bottle-fermented, as in Champagne, but the cheaper brands are either made by the Charmat process, i.e., tank-fermented or with carbonic acid gas pumped into them.

Q. **Where are the vineyards and wineries of Australia?**

A. More than two-thirds of them are in South Australia, then, a long way down, comes New South Wales, and then Victoria. They are the three oldest and largest wine-producing States of Australia. Western Australia, however, has made much progress of late years and is not far behind Victoria. There are a few vineyards in Queensland, but the climate of that State is not favourable to viticulture.

Q. **Which are the chief wine-producing areas of South Australia?**

A. There are seven wine-producing areas in South Australia as follows:

(1)   The Adelaide Plains and Foothills vineyards, the oldest in the state and the nearest to Adelaide, at Magill, Burnside and Modbury, north-east of Adelaide; Glenelg, Glen Osmond, and the O'Halloran Hill to the south-west.

(2)   The Southern District, from 12 to 25 miles south of Adelaide, with Reynella, the Morphett Vale with the Emu Winery, the McLaren Vale with Tintara, Seaview and other wineries.

(3)   The Barossa Valley some 20 miles long, from 30 to 50 miles from Adelaide and the undulating country surrounding the North Para River and its tributaries; also the Eden Valley. Chief towns are Tanunda, Nuriootpa, Greenock, Angaston; also Lyndoch and Williamstown. Smith's Yalumba, Gramp's Orlando, and Seppelt's at Seppeltsfield are the largest of many Barossa wineries.

(4)   The Clare area, a hilly area some 80 miles north of Adelaide, with Buring & Sobels Winery at Watervale.

(5)   The Upper Murray River irrigation area, much the largest wine-producing district of the state from 100 to 140 miles north-east of Adelaide with important settlements at Cadell, Waikerie, Kingston, Barmera, Berri, Loxton, and Renmark.

(6)   The Coonwarra area over 200 miles south-west of Adelaide, the southernmost vineyards of Australia and of the world where the Rouge-Homme winery and a number of others produce some of the best dry red wines of Australia.

(7)   The Langhorne's Creek area, the smallest of all, 35 miles south-east of Adelaide, on the Bremer River, where the Bleasdale vineyard was first planted by Frank Potts.

Q. **Which are the chief wine-producing areas of New South Wales?**

A. There are but three important wine-producing areas now left in New South Wales:

(1)   The Hunter Valley vineyards, some of them the oldest in Australia, like Dalwood, near Branxton, and most of them in the nearby Pokolbin district, such as Mount Pleasant, Ben Ean, Tulloch's, Tyrrell's, Oakvale, Bellevue, Glendora, Sunshine, etc. The large Wyborn Park vineyard, near Musselbrook, is about 18 miles west of Pokolbin.

(2)   Corowa is a western frontier township and its vineyards along-

173

side the left bank of the Murray River face those of Wangunyah, in Victoria: two of the more important are Southern Cross and Felton.

(3) The Griffith district is a long way to the north, in the valley of the Murrumbidgee: the township is completely surrounded by vineyards which are irrigated by the water of the Burrunjunc Reservoir.

Q. **Which are the chief wine-making areas of Victoria?**
A. There are only four areas of any importance in Victoria:

(1) The north-east vineyards or Rutherglen district which stretches to the Murray River, at Wangunyah. Many of the vineyards destroyed by the phylloxera at the end of the nineteenth century have been replanted and are flourishing at Fairfield (Morris), Wangunyah (All Saints), and a number of others. Although the vineyards of Milawa, some 10 miles from Wangaratta, a long way west of Rutherglen are not in the north-east corner of Victoria, they produce wines of the same standard as those of Rutherglen.

(2) The Goulburn vineyards some 35 miles north of Melbourne owe their fame chiefly to the wines of Château Tahbilk which were first planted in 1860 and are still among the best red and white table or beverage wines of Australia.

(3) The Great Western vineyards which are not considerable in extent now but are reputed, as they have been for many years past, for the sparkling wines made there at the Seppelt Winery.

(4) The Mildura irrigation area on the Murray River: its vineyards are the most recent in Victoria, but they produce a greater tonnage of grapes than the others. Mildura is the name of the organisation responsible for the care of the vineyards as well as the making and marketing of their wines, spirits and dried fruit.

New Zealand

Q. **Are there any vineyards in New Zealand?**
A. There are over 1,000 acres of vineyards in New Zealand and their average annual production is about 1¼ million gallons of wine.

Q. **Where are the New Zealand vineyards?**

A. All the vineyards of New Zealand from which wine is made commercially are in the North Island, chiefly in the Henderson district near Auckland, where they produce some 650,000 gallons of wine annually, and in the Hawke's Bay area, near Napier, where they produce some 550,000 gallons of wine annually.

Q. **What are the wines of New Zealand like?**
A. Practically every type of wine is made in New Zealand, dry and sweet, still and sparkling, table wines and dessert wines, most of them somewhat similar to the wines of like types made in Australia.

U.S.A.

Q. **When were wine-making grapes first planted in California?**
A. The first European (*vitis vinifera*) grapes to be planted on the Western Coast of the Spanish Main were those of the San Francisco Xavier Mission of Baja California (Mexico). They were planted, according to tradition, by Father Juan Ugarte, a Jesuit priest, before the end of the seventeenth century. Vines were first planted in Alta California, and the Southern California of today, at a number of Franciscan Missions, along the king's highway — *El camino real* — during the eighteenth century.

Q. **What kind of grapes did the Franciscan friars plant in California?**
A. The first grape which the Spanish Franciscan friars planted in California was a *vitis vinifera* grape which bore a large number of big clusters with loosely set, medium size, brownish-red grapes known as the Mission grape.

Q. **What type of wine is made from the Mission grape?**
A. The Mission grape is a low quality type of grape, lacking in acidity, but the Franciscan friars apparently made two different types of wine from the Mission grape, a dry sacramental wine and a sweet dessert wine which was called Angelica.

Q. **When was wine made commercially in California?**
A. Vines were grown and wine was made commercially in California during the second half of the nineteenth century, after the American

occupation of the country, in 1846/47. A surprisingly large number of the immigrants who flooded California at the time, planted vines mostly near Los Angeles, and there were 6 million vines in production, in 1860.

Q. **Who was Count Agoston Haraszthy?**

A. Count Agoston Haraszthy was a Hungarian nobleman who deserves the name of Father of Californian viticulture. It was he who selected in Europe, in 1862, and brought to California, all the best species which have been cultivated ever since with conspicuous success.

Q. **How did prohibition affect California?**

A. Prohibition was a major disaster for California. There was but little wine allowed to be made for sacramental purposes, but all sorts of poor quality vines of the Alicante Bouschet type replaced the better wine-making vines and produced legal 'table' grapes for which the demand had become prodigious; many more vines were also grown for drying grapes.

Q. **What has happened since prohibition?**

A. Since the Repeal of Prohibition, in 1933, a considerable and successful effort has been made to restock the vineyards of California with some of the better quality grapes selected for their suitability to the soil and climate of individual vineyards.

Q. **What is the climate of California?**

A. The climate of the vineyards of California varies greatly according to the location of the vineyards, from cold and temperate, north and south of San Francisco, to sub-tropical heat and drought south of Los Angeles.

Q. **Which are the wines mostly made in California?**

A. About two-thirds of all the wines made in California are fortified wines with from 18% to 21% of alcohol. A small proportion of these wines of the Sherry and Port types are quality dessert wines, but the great majority are made from common grapes and marketed much too soon after being made to be any good.

Q. **What are the other California wines?**

A. About 20% of the whole are red table wines, 5% white wines, both still, beverage wines, most of them of very fair quality, being made from some of the best European grapes such as Cabernet Sauvignon and Pinot Noir for the reds, Pinot Chardonnay and Riesling for the whites.

Q. **Do they make any sparkling wines in California?**

A. They make three types of sparkling wines in California, the best and dearest are made by the *Méthode Champenoise*, or bottle fermented; the next best are made by the Charmat process or tank fermented; and the third, which are of a very inferior kind, are carbonated wines. Most of the California sparkling wines are white, but there are some red ones also.

Q. **Which are the principal wine-grapes counties of California?**

A. The principal wine-grapes counties of California are, from north to south, as follows:
Northern: Mendocino, Sonoma, Napa, Solano, Yuba, Sutter, Placer, Solo, and Sacramento, north of San Francisco. Alameda, Santa Clara, and Santa Cruz, south of San Francisco.
Central: San Joaquin, Stanislaus, Merced, Madera, Fresno, Tulare, Kings, and Kern.
Coastal: San Benito, Monterey, and San Luis Obispo.
Southern: Los Angeles, San Bernardino, Riverside, and San Diego.

Q. **Which are the names mostly used for the marketing of California fortified wines?**

A. Fortified wines are mostly marketed under the following names:
Port and *Sherry* made to look like their prototypes of Portugal and Spain; a few, the best of them, do bear some likeness to the real Port and Sherry;
Madeira, Malaga, Tokay, which may be good, bad or indifferent wines but make no pretence to resemble the European wines of the same names;
Muscatel is no approximation of any European wine, but a sweet, fortified California wine made from Muscat grapes of good or not so good quality which accounts for wide differences in the appeal of different Muscatels;
Angelica is no wine at all but a *mistella*, that is grape juice, the

177

fermentation of which has been stopped by alcohol. The name, however, is sometimes given to new wine the fermentation of which has been checked after it had started fermenting.

Q. **Which are the names used for the marketing of California table wines?**

A. Most red table wines are marketed under the names of Claret, Burgundy or Zinfandel, the last name being that of a red grape from which a Claret type of wine is made. White table wines are mostly marketed as Sauterne, Dry Sauterne or Haut Sauterne (the final 's' of the French Sauternes always missing). Some wineries market their sweetest, and presumably best 'Sauterne' as *Château*. There are also white wines which are sold under the names of Chablis, Hock, Moselle, or Riesling.

Q. **Which are the names used for the marketing of California sparkling wines?**

A. California sparkling wines are marketed as Champagne, when white, and as sparkling Burgundy when red.

Q. **What is the proportion of American wine made in California?**

A. The wine production of California is roughly 90% of all the wine made in the United States of America.

Q. **Is wine made on a commercial scale in any of the American States other than California?**

A. There are a dozen States other than California in which there are vineyards and where some wine is made commercially, mostly, however, on a small scale. The only States where viticulture and wine-making are really important are the States of New York, Ohio, and Missouri, with Kansas, North Carolina, and New Jersey coming next.

Q. **What are the types of wine mostly made in those States?**

A. They are mostly beverage table wines as well as sparkling wines, more especially from the vineyards of the Finger Lakes of New York State and from New Jersey.

Chile

Q. **Are there many vineyards in Chile?**

A. There are many vineyards in Chile, chiefly upon the lower slopes of the Andes in the Santiago Province.

Q. **How important is the wine production of Chile?**

A. The wine production of Chile varies from 9 to 12 million gallons of wine per annum, about one-third of the wine production of the Argentine.

Q. **Are the wines of Chile comparable to those of the Argentine?**

A. Most wines of Chile are of much finer quality than the majority of the Argentine wines.

Q. **Why should this be?**

A. This is chiefly due to the fact that the vineyards of Chile are not irrigated like those of the Argentine, and many of them were originally planted by Basque *vignerons* from the Spanish and French sides of the Pyrenees whose descendants appear to have inherited great pride in the quality of their wines.

Q. **Are any of the wines of Chile available in Great Britain and the U.S.A?**

A. A number of the red and white still wines of Chile are highly appreciated in the U.S.A., chiefly the white wines. In Great Britain there are not many wine-merchants who import and sell the wines of Chile, but those who do can rightly claim that they are the peers of wines of the same type from European vineyards; Chilean wines are usually cheaper and better value than many equivalent European wines.

APPENDIX: VINTAGE CHART

0 = No Good   7 = The Best

YEAR	CHAMPAGNE	WHITE BURGUNDY	SAUTERNES	RHINE	RHONE	BURGUNDY	CLARET	PORT
1964	7	6	3	6	7	6	6	4
1963	4	5	2	4	5	4	4	6
1962	6	5	6	6	6	5	6	5
1961	6	6	5	5	5	6	6	4
1960	4	3	4	5	5	5	4	7
1959	7	7	7	7	6	6	7	3
1958	5	4	5	5	6	4	5	5
1957	2	5	3	5	4	5	5	5
1956	4	3	4	3	5	2	3	2
1955	7	6	6	5	7	6	6	7
1954	3	4	3	3	5	4	4	5
1953	7	7	7	7	6	6	7	5
1952	7	6	6	6	7	7	6	4
1951	2	3	3	2	4	3	3	3
1950	3	6	4	5	6	4	6	6
1949	6	6	5	7	6	6	7	4
1948	4	5	4	5	4	5	6	7
1947	7	7	7	6	7	7	7	7
1946	3	5	3	4	4	4	3	5
1945	6	6	7	6	6	7	6	7

0 = No Good   7 = The Best

YEAR	CHAMPAGNE	WHITE BURGUNDY	SAUTERNES	RHINE	RHONE	BURGUNDY	CLARET	PORT
1944	3	2	4	3	3	2	4	4
1943	5	6	6	5	6	5	5	5
1942	5	4	4	5	5	3	3	6
1941	4	1	0	2	3	1	1	4
1940	3	1	3	3	2	2	3	5
1939	2	2	2	3	3	2	2	3
1938	4	4	3	4	5	3	4	5
1937	5	7	7	6	6	5	5	4
1936	2	4	3	1	5	2	3	3
1935	3	5	2	5	3	4	2	7
1934	6	6	5	7	5	6	6	6
1933	5	5	2	6	6	6	4	4
1932	2	2	0	3	2	2	0	1
1931	2	1	2	2	0	0	2	6
1930	1	3	0	3	1	1	1	2
1929	7	7	7	5	7	6	7	3
1928	7	6	6	1	5	5	6	1
1927	1	2	2	4	6	1	1	7
1926	6	6	5	3	4	6	5	3
1925	2	3	3	4	5	2	3	3

INDEX OF WINES AND VINEYARDS
and places of origin

Names beginning with an article (eg. La) are under that.

Names beginning with a preposition are under following words (except d').